COURT IN SESSION

By JETHRO KOLLER LIEBERMAN
Introduction by JUDGE KENNETH B. KEATING

STERLING PUBLISHING CO., Inc.   New York

OTHER BOOKS OF INTEREST

Boys' Life of John F. Kennedy

The 51 Capitals of the U.S.A.

Government at Work

Picture Book of Famous Immigrants

Picture Book of The Presidents

DEDICATION

For Susan

ACKNOWLEDGMENTS

The author wishes to thank Henry Putzel, Jr., Reporter of Decisions of the Supreme Court of the United States, for his reading of the chapter on the Supreme Court and his aid in obtaining pictures, and the following people for their valuable aid, advice and suggestions: David M. Brodsky, Sandor Frankel, A. Van C. Lanckton, Elizabeth Lieberman, J. Ben Lieberman, Jack T. Litman, Bernard Novick, Jonathan A. Small, and Jon M. Van Dyke. The author and publisher wish to thank the Edward C. Thompson Company for their aid in charting the courts, and the Port of New York Authority and the White House for supplying photographs.

1458853

Contents

Written Contracts . . . Bilateral and Unilateral Contracts . . . CRIMINAL LAW . . . STATUTORY SUITS . . . REMEDIES . . . Injunction . . . Temporary Restraining Order . . . Specific Performance . . . Reformation . . . Rescission . . . Restitution . . . Garnishment . . . Attachment . . . Civil Contempt . . . SANCTIONS . . . Fines . . . Jail . . . Capital Punishment . . . Corporal Punishment . . . Parole . . . Probation . . . Suspended Sentence . . . Criminal Contempt . . . PROHIBITIONS AGAINST LAW SUITS

Introduction

I first met Jethro Lieberman in Washington during the summer of 1963, when he worked on my staff in the United States Senate. I know of his intense interest in informing young people about the law.

In this book he explains his picture of what happens in civil and criminal cases, how our court system functions, and what the average person should know about the law. He discusses the arguments, pro and con, on such subjects as punishment, assessment of damages, indictments and injunctions, constitutional law, rights and freedoms, and the other terms which the untrained person continually finds in the daily papers, if not in actual legal controversy.

I highly recommend this book as an informative story for any young person, but especially for young people contemplating a career in the law or in politics.

Kenneth B. Keating

*State of New York,
Court of Appeals,*

Part I: The Case of the Missing House

It all seemed simple enough at the outset: Mr. S (the Seller) wanted to sell his house, and Mr. B (the Buyer) wanted to buy it. After some discussion they agreed to make a deal, settled on a price ($25,000), and decided which rooms were first to be painted by Mr. S. To "bind" each other to this agreement, Mr. S and Mr. B signed a "contract" which they wrote themselves. It stated, among other things, that Mr. B promised to pay Mr. S $25,000 on a date six weeks off, and that the seller promised to give the buyer a "deed" to the house and the land at that time. If they had not put the "oral agreement" in writing in the state where they lived, either "party" (side) to the contract would have been legally entitled to withdraw from the deal later on.

THE ACCIDENT

Although no money had changed hands, Mr. S was relieved that the contract had been signed. At a party on the other side of town that night he was pleased to tell his friends: "I finally sold my house."

But while he was enjoying himself at the party, tragedy struck. The house next door to Mr. S's burst into flames, and the fire roared through the block. By the time the firemen arrived Mr. S's house had burned to the ground. Mr. S returned later that evening to the smoldering rubble of ashes and bricks that had been his home.

One question kept recurring to Mr. S during the next few hours as he sought refuge in a hotel: who owned the house at the time of its destruction? If the house still belonged to him, he would almost certainly have to bear the loss of $25,000. If Mr. B legally owned the house, however, the loss would lie on his shoulders.

The next morning Mr. S went to see his attorney to discuss the problem. Mr. S pointed out that his fire insurance covered only the contents of the house, but that the house itself was not insured. His lawyer was of the opinion that Mr. S need not worry: the contract had been signed and the house had been sold. Mr. S then phoned Mr. B, who lived in the next town, to tell him about the fire. Mr. B said that he had read about the catastrophe in the newspaper and that he was "terribly sorry" Mr. S had incurred such a loss. Mr. S was a little surprised:

"But it was your house; we made a written agreement and the house was sold to you. Didn't you cover it with insurance?"

"No, of course I didn't," Mr. B replied, "since I haven't yet paid you any money. Look, I really don't think I should have to pay you anything since I can't get the house. Let me talk to my lawyer and call you back."

Mr. B's attorney was disturbed.

"You *shouldn't* have to pay the money, but I'm not sure that a court won't hold against you. After all, Mr. S is being perfectly reasonable. He *did* make the contract with you, and it would have been binding if the house had not burned down. It may still be binding."

THE NEGOTIATIONS

After some discussion, Mr. B's lawyer advised him to "settle" the dispute with Mr. S while they were still on friendly terms and before anyone talked about going to court.

"If you go to court you may lose the whole case and have to pay Mr. S the $25,000. It's better to offer him a smaller amount, say the value of the land, in return for which he will agree not to sue you. You will at least get the land. That way you'll save the time, trouble, and cost of a legal suit and you won't run the danger of losing," Mr. B's lawyer explained.

So Mr. B called Mr. S and offered him $10,000 for the land as settlement. But Mr. S refused the offer, preferring—on the advice of his lawyer—to take his chances that "litigation" (suing in court) would enable him to get the entire amount.

The next day Mr. S received a letter from Mr. B repeating the offer: $10,000 in return for a deed to the land and an agreement not to sue. Mr. S took the letter to his lawyer, where it sat for a few days while the attorney acted on other business that needed his immediate attention. About a week later a young associate in his law firm gave Mr. S's lawyer a "memorandum" (report) on what the law of the state was concerning such an incident and what he thought a court might decide. The gist of the memo was that Mr. S had a fairly good chance of winning the lawsuit, so at a meeting with Mr. S, his lawyer advised him not to accept the $10,000, but to sue if Mr. B refused to pay the full $25,000.

Mr. S thought it over and took his lawyer's advice. He wrote to Mr. B, rejecting his offer, and asking again for full payment in return for the deed to be given at the time set by the contract. Mr. B again refused, and Mr. S asked his lawyer, Mr. P, to start a suit in the local county court.

THE LAW SUIT

The function of the court in our society is to serve as a peaceful and impartial chamber in which disputes can be settled or adjudged according to established rules. Our society depends on the fact that millions of contracts can be made annually with a good chance that all but a very few will be carried out smoothly. Some institution (in our society, the court and the lawyers who are licensed to practice) must be able to prevent or end disruptions which occur when contracts are "breached" (broken). Even though maintaining the court system costs taxpayers a great deal of money, it is the best way known to man of keeping peace among citizens.

Some four weeks after the fire, Mr. S's lawyer drew up a "complaint," a document presenting the dispute and the grounds for the suit, and asking that the court order Mr. B to pay $25,000 to Mr. S in return for the deed. Lawyer P (for "plaintiff," the complainant) filed it at the courthouse. When the court received the complaint, it dispatched an authorized official to "serve" Mr. B with a "summons" directing him to file an "answer" to the charges made against him. The court also sent to Mr. B a copy of Mr. S's complaint. The summons is an essential part of our democratic legal process, since it legally informs a person of a complaint made against him.

Mr. B's attorney, Lawyer D (the defendant's lawyer) thought the complaint as written was unclear. He couldn't tell if Lawyer P was contending that the contract said *explicitly* (distinctly, by its very words) that Mr. B should bear the loss, or whether Lawyer P was saying merely that he thought the contract *should* have that effect. Therefore, Lawyer D went to the courthouse and "made a motion" (a request) for a more definite statement from Mr. S and his attorney. If this case had taken place in another state, Lawyer D, after answering the complaint, would have asked instead for a "bill of particulars" (a written statement from the plaintiff, who made the original complaint, explaining the charges in greater detail).

The court granted the motion of the defendant's lawyer, so Lawyer P was obliged to submit a more detailed written statement. Lawyer P explained that he thought that even though the contract did not state *explicitly* that Mr. B should bear the loss, that was clearly *implied* and he felt that legally the contract should have that effect.

Thereupon lawyer D filed his answer, admitting the facts which the plaintiff had set forth, but denying that they meant Mr. B owed Mr. S the contract price. Lawyer D then made a motion in court (that is, asked) for "summary judgment." In other words, he wanted the judge, on the basis of the facts in the complaint and answer, together with such supporting documents as the contract, to declare that his client, Mr. B, had no legal obligation to pay. Lawyer D set a day for a hearing of the motion, and served notice of the motion and the day on Lawyer P. Prior to the hearing day, Lawyer P served "answering papers" on Lawyer D in which he contested Mr. B's right to summary judgment. Lawyer D then submitted a reply. The original of the papers all went to the judge.

In preparing these papers, the attorneys busied themselves "checking out" the law: they studied various books of reports to find out what courts had said in the past when faced with similar cases, and tried to discover whether the legislature of the state (or other states) had enacted any laws relevant to the dispute. The judge did similar research in his "chambers" (office) when he was not in the actual courtroom deciding on other cases.

MOTION DAY

Finally, a few weeks after the fire occurred, motion day arrived, and the lawyers went to court for the hearing. The judge conducted the informal discussion in his chambers. Present were the plaintiff, the defendant, their lawyers, and a court stenographer. It quickly became evident that the issue was simple: Was Mr. B the actual owner of the house at the time of the fire (and thereby liable) or could he have the contract "rescinded" (canceled) because of the fire, thereby "escaping" from the agreement? Both lawyers agreed on the material facts: they told the judge that they were not disputing what had happened. They disagreed only as to the legal consequences. After reading the contract and discussing its terms with the lawyers, the judge made a formal ruling that the case need not go to trial, since a trial is necessary only to determine matters of fact. Because the dispute was one of law only, the judge felt able to order a summary judgment. From a reading of the "pleadings" (complaint and answer), the contract, and from the facts, the judge stated that he would be able to give a summary, or quick, decision. "Summary" does not mean the decision is given by the judge off the top of his head; it isn't. The judge had considered the problem in advance of the conference, and now he asked the lawyers to outline the reasons for their opinions as to the law.

Mr. S's lawyer said that *not* to enforce the contract would mean that a seller would not in the future be able to know when his house was sold and make plans accordingly; that the signing of the contract must have meant *something*; otherwise it would not have been signed. He also pointed out that the majority of states have a rule which puts the loss on the buyer. Mr. B's lawyer argued, on the other hand, that since there was no house left to buy, and since Mr. B didn't want the land without the house, it would be unfair to make him pay for nothing. He pointed out that some states have rules that make the seller bear the loss.

SUMMARY JUDGMENT

Then the judge rendered his judgment. He began by saying that it was a difficult case and that to his knowledge a similar case had never arisen in this state before. The judge pointed out that the decision was especially difficult not only because both Mr. S and Mr. B had acted fairly and honestly, but because there was a good deal of right in each of their positions.

However, the judge decided that Mr. S, the seller, was more entitled to the money. Thus he denied Mr. B's motion for summary judgment and granted Mr. S's motion, ruling that Mr. B would have to pay the $25,000 in return for the deed to the land. Mr. S, the plaintiff, had won. The judge instructed the clerk of the court to enter judgment for plaintiff in the amount of $25,000 in a special court book kept for the purpose.

If the material facts had been in dispute, the judge would not have rendered summary judgment. Instead, he would have set a date for a trial of the facts of the case. Had he ordered a trial, the attorneys would have become very busy gathering facts and witnesses. They might have mailed papers to the parties and witnesses asking for written answers to specific questions. These papers are called "interrogatories." The attorneys might "take a deposition" of a party or witness: the party or witness would be put under oath and would have to answer questions asked orally by the opposing attorney; the answers would be written down and made a part of the formal record of the case. Prior to trial, the judge might call a pre-trial conference to simplify the issues and to try to resolve the differences between the parties and bring about a settlement. But none of this was necessary in our case.

APPEALING THE CASE

Was this the end of the case? Far from it. Mr. B's lawyer did not give up. A losing party who feels he has grounds to show he has not received a completely fair deal from the trial judge can "appeal" his case by taking it to a higher court for review. "Appellate courts" exist as part of the legal system, but the litigants have to help themselves—the appellate court will not start action by itself. Law in America is based on the so-called "adversary system": each party is, in effect, pitted in a struggle with the other, and judges wait for cases to be brought to them. This is as true at the trial level as at the appellate level. No one is forced—or even encouraged—to appeal, but this recourse is available for those who want it.

Mr. B's lawyer told him that it was not at all certain the judge was wrong. In fact, he said, the odds were not great that Mr. B would win on appeal. On the other hand, Lawyer D thought he could argue convincingly that the trial judge made the wrong decision, so that the expense and trouble of the appeal might be worth the gamble. However, it *was* a gamble, and Mr. B would have to decide.

Because $25,000 was at stake, Mr. B decided to risk a little more money on the appeal. Lawyer D then notified the trial court of the decision to appeal to the state supreme court, the next and highest state court. Upon receipt of this notice, the trial judge who had "sat" on the case notified the plaintiff (Mr. S) of the defendant's appeal. He then sent the "record" (the petition for appeal, the pleadings, a copy of the contract, and a written statement of the judgment and the reasons for it) to the state supreme court. The clerk of that court noted on the "judicial calendar" a date four months away as the time when the supreme court judges would hear the case.

Appellate courts rule only on whether the trial judge has made a mistake. Do trial judges make mistakes? Of course they do. The trial judge *decides what the law is* (and, as we shall see, instructs the jury when there is a jury trial). It may seem that judges can simply make their decisions by reading the law as it is written, but *interpretation* of the meaning of the words is often the bulk of the law. Nearly all "statutes" (laws passed by the legislature) can be read with different meanings; it is the difficult lot of the trial judge to interpret the law according to the case and circumstances before him. In addition, many laws are not statutes at all, but part of so-called "unwritten" laws. "Unwritten" is a misleading term, for in fact unwritten laws have been written down by the judges who made them. In our case, there was no statute which said that the buyer had to pay the seller, but the judge decided there was an unwritten law (called a "rule") to that effect.

HOLDINGS AND DICTA

A rule is really a judge-made law. (The term "rule" is also used to refer to the procedures by which the court operates; for example, the Rules of the Court guide attorneys as to how and when to file papers, etc.) Judgments handed down by courts are called rulings or "holdings." A holding is made as a case is being decided, and can apply only to cases with the same facts. Thus, the holding in our present case would not have been the same if Mr. B, for example, had only agreed to the contract orally and had not signed the written contract.

It was the trial judge's responsibility to decide which previous holdings in the state's courts applied to the case before him. Since the losing party was unhappy with the decision and made an appeal, the appellate court was empowered to examine the case and determine whether the trial judge accurately interpreted the law. If the trial judge interpreted wrongly, the appellate court might "remand" (return) the case to the lower court for a new trial, or, the appellate court might make the final judgment itself. Whether to remand or decide depends upon the circumstances of the case.

Occasionally, a trial judge may make a ruling that is called a "dictum" because it does not deal with the issues in question. For example, if the judge had incidentally said, in his ruling, that Mr. S could not have been awarded the $25,000 if a different kind of contract had been signed, this kind of irrelevant statement would be called a "dictum," since it had nothing to do with the case at hand. If a statement otherwise sounds like a holding, but is not logically needed to reach a just decision, or does not deal specifically with the issue involved, it is a dictum, not a holding.

THE COMMON LAW

Over a period of centuries, holdings in the British-American judicial tradition have been condensed into "principles" which have been generally approved and accepted by judges as fair and just. This set of principles is called the "common law" because it is held in common by all judges in a state.

Judges follow these ancient rules. What can the holdings in cases years or centuries old have to do with the cases of today? The answer comes from the oldest and most fundamental policy of the British-American legal tradition: once a court has decided that a particular rule applies to a certain set of facts, it applies the same rule in all cases involving substantially the same facts. This policy is called "*stare decisis*" (from the Latin for "to stand by decided matters").

Stare decisis is an important factor in the maintenance of a legally just society. Since a person knows that the rule in a previous case can be relied on as a "precedent," he can carry out personal actions and make business decisions, secure in the knowledge that what was legal yesterday will probably be legal today and tomorrow.

This does not mean that the common law cannot be changed. The legislature can pass a statute abolishing or modifying a common law rule. The courts, too, can change the common law if they find a holding in a previous case unjust or harsh. Judges will sometimes overrule old precedents, when changing conditions in society require it, in an effort to see that justice is done.

Common law rules and judicial interpretations of statutes are written down as they are announced, so that lawyers everywhere can follow them and their clients can rely on judicial precedents. The judges' "opinions" (which state the holdings and reasoning in a case) are printed in official books called "reports." The federal courts and most state courts publish their own official reports, but private companies also print and publish the opinions of every case decided in the high level appellate courts. It is in these reports that the "unwritten laws" are written.

In a trial court there is only one judge, but in an appellate court there are several. In the topmost (supreme) court of a state, there are usually five or seven judges, who act as a panel: they almost always consider all cases together, and do not usually delegate different cases to different judges. The judges do not have to be unanimous in their decisions—a majority decides.

PREPARING FOR THE HEARING

The preparation for a hearing in an appellate court is different from preparation for trial. The facts are already known and will not be argued. But the facts must be "written up" for the appellate judges. Each lawyer must use his ingenuity in presenting the facts, so that while he is honest, he also catches the sympathy of the court. It is often crucial to make the judges think that your side is the deserving one; if they think you *ought* to win, they will usually be able to find a reason that will let you win.

The lawyers for each party must do the bulk of the work, even though the appellate judges often look up the law themselves. A lawyer must think of and use every helpful argument in favor of his client. In doing this properly, he anticipates the arguments the other side will use. In practice, this means a lawyer must really be able to argue both sides of any case. A lawyer's style, his knowledge of the facts, and his ability to answer questions quickly can make a big difference on appeal. No one, not even a judge, can fail to be impressed with a man who has command of his case.

In preparing for the oral "argument" (presentation before the judges), a lawyer "researches" the law of his case thoroughly. He will find the official reports in his office, the courthouse, or a law library. There are hundreds of volumes covering literally thousands of cases for each state. Normally, the lawyers examine only the cases of the state in which the court sits, but sometimes, when a particular situation has never arisen in a state before, as in our present case, the judges will want to know about the laws and holdings in other states. The lawyer's problem is to find the appropriate laws and holdings.

As can be imagined, researching a case can be slow and tedious. Recently, electronic computers have been enlisted by lawyers. With the aid of the computer's enormous memory capacity, cases can be located quickly.

In addition, there are thousands of articles in professional journals and in treatises, legal encyclopedias, and other books. Of course, both lawyers in the present case had already done the groundwork when they prepared for the pre-trial conference at the county courthouse. But now they had to dig deeper still. They found articles in a treatise called *The American Law of Property*, in Tiffany's *Real Property*, in Williston's *Contracts*. They read and argued from an article titled "Equitable Conversion by Contract" written by a Chief Justice of the United States. They cited cases from Missouri, Maryland, Massachusetts, and even England. The reading was dense and heavy, but crucial to the arguments.

THE BRIEF

When a lawyer has finished his research, he prepares a "brief." A brief is just what it sounds like: a concise statement of the facts of the case and the legal arguments involved. Sometimes a brief will be as short as 10 pages;

sometimes it will contain 100 pages or more. Since the brief is the judges' first encounter with the case, it should be as short and direct as possible. The longer it is, the less inclined the judges will be to read it. Who wants to read 100 dull, dry pages of legal arguments? Judges would much rather read ten 10-page briefs. The lawyer's task is to convince the court that his client should win, not to impress the judges with his extensive knowledge.

On a day scheduled by the court, both lawyers submit their briefs to a clerk of the court. The judges receive copies, and each lawyer receives a copy of his opponent's brief. Sometimes, depending on the state, the court will order the lawyers to file "reply briefs." These are very short briefs which take issue with the arguments presented in the opposing lawyer's first brief. A shorter time is allowed in which to prepare and submit these.

THE ORAL ARGUMENT

After the judges have had a chance to study the briefs, the day for "argument" arrives. Each lawyer is allowed a short time—almost never more than one hour and usually less—to present his side of the case. The first side to argue is the "appellant," in the present case Mr. B, the defendant, who lost in the trial court.

A lawyer appealing a case has two basic strategies in both his brief and his argument. He must try to convince the appellate judges that previous cases support his side or that previous cases are wrong and should be reversed. If he can find really clear-cut cases that support his client with holdings that are exactly in point, a lawyer can rely on the first strategy. But if the meaning of past cases is unclear, or if there are no cases directly in point, he must try to convince the court that the law *should* support his client. If previous cases are against him, he can "distinguish" them, that is, show that they are different or distinct from the case at hand and that they are therefore not relevant or "controlling." He can argue that what seems to be a holding in an adverse case is really a mere dictum and that the judges should therefore disregard the case. Or, he can argue that the adverse cases are unjust and should be reversed. The opposing lawyer will of course argue to the contrary, so it will be up to the judges to select the most compelling arguments.

Mr. B's attorney, Lawyer D, stood facing the black-robed judges, who were sitting behind the "bench" (the long desk across one end of the courtroom). Time was limited because many cases were to be argued that day. Lawyer D began to explain his position, but in a few minutes he was interrupted in the middle of a sentence by a judge who began, "Now, counsel, is it your position that . . .?" (Lawyers are often referred to as "counsel" since it is a lawyer's function to give counsel to both client and court.) Many difficult, often sharp, questions are asked, as the judges try to get to the root of the case as quickly as possible. Lawyer D never finished his prepared statement, which merely expanded on his brief. Instead, he had to answer the judges' questions during almost all his allotted time.

Since the judges' questions were pointed, it was a sign that they had read the briefs carefully and had been thinking about the case. The good lawyer turns the judges' questions to his own advantage, for the questions are a clue to how the judges view the case. This is important, obviously, because impressions and distortions will affect a judge's decision. The lawyer who is able to analyze a judge's question, even while he is answering it, and spot impressions and distortions, can often correct a judge's mistaken notions and win the case for his client.

When Lawyer D finished, Lawyer P, Mr. S's attorney, had his turn. Neither the "appellee" (the party who had won in the trial court) nor the "appellant" (the party who had lost and was appealing) needed to be in court.

When Lawyer P finished stating his case, Lawyer D was given a very short time—no more than five minutes—for "rebuttal." During this period he tried to convince the judges that Lawyer P was wrong. Then the case was in the hands of the judges.

You may have noticed that the lawyers do all the work in an appeal. That is because they are trained in the law and have the legal vocabulary and knowledge to cope with the questions of the judges.

During the next weeks, out of court, the judges discussed the case with each other and did their own research. (In some courts judges have the help of young "law clerks" who are chosen by the judges on the basis of their law school records.) Months after the day of argument, the judges assembled and voted on the case. A majority of the judges voted to reverse the judgment of the lower court! This meant that Mr. B had won.

THE DECISION

The chief judge wrote the "majority opinion," a statement with reasons that appears first in the official report volume. Any other judge who agrees with the majority, but for reasons other than those given in the written majority opinion, can write a "concurring opinion." Any judge who disagrees with the majority decision can write a "dissenting opinion," saying why he disagrees. There may be one or more concurring and dissenting opinions. All are printed in the reports after the majority opinion.

On a pre-determined "decision day," the judges assembled in open court with the attorneys present and the chief judge read the majority opinion: "The contract of sale here involved contained no provision as to who assumed the risk of loss occasioned by a destruction of the house, or for protecting the house by insurance." He next discussed the five different rules which different states had developed as to who should bear the loss and commended "the learned trial judge for his opinion in a difficult case." Because the state supreme court had never considered such a case before, the chief judge said the court was adopting the "Massachusetts rule" (borrowed from that state) which puts the loss on the seller. Said the chief judge: "The reason for the Massachusetts rule is that an order to make the buyer pay is based on what is equitable; and it is not equitable to make a vendee (buyer) pay the vendor (seller) for something the vendor cannot give him." In other words, to make the buyer pay would have been unfair, and the court will not order an unjust act to be performed. Three of the seven judges dissented, however, and their opinions showed how close and difficult the decision was.

Since the state supreme court reversed the lower court, the case was remanded to the county court, with instructions to the trial judge to erase the judgment for plaintiff and enter a "final judgment" for the defendant, dismissing plaintiff's complaint and rescinding the contract. The court also ordered Mr. S (since he had lost) to pay the costs of appeal. These included costs of preparing the record and preparation of various documents and papers, but they did not include Mr. B's lawyer's fee. Each party, except in rare cases, must pay his own lawyer's fee.

THE RULE

From now on, when a similar case arises in the same state, the trial judge will know that under the state's law a seller must bear the loss if there is no insurance, even though the majority of states may hold the other way. But it is not likely that cases of the same kind will come again to the courts in that state, for, since lawyers follow all recent decisions of their state supreme court, they will take the new rule into account when they draft contracts for their clients.

Of course, if two persons make a contract without consulting lawyers, they probably will not know about the rule and may find themselves in a similar dispute. Then the lawyers they eventually hire will advise them to settle out of court.

Now, nine months after the fire, is this the end? In this case, it is. In about one-quarter of the states, more than one level of appellate courts serves the people; a case can first go to an intermediate court and then to the state supreme court. As we shall see, some kinds of state cases, though not this one, can be appealed to the United States Supreme Court.

The Judgment of Solomon.

Part II: The Case of the Stolen Money

THE HOLDUP

Wednesday was pay day at the corner drug store, and shortly after two in the afternoon the money was brought from the bank to the cashier-manager's desk to be distributed to the store's employees. Suddenly a man wearing a light blue overcoat and dark sunglasses burst into the store. He walked to the cashier's desk near the front, waving a gun at the frightened customers. "All right now, nobody moves, nobody gets hurt," he said. While 15 customers looked on, the robber demanded the payroll money. "All right, Smith," he said to the cashier-manager, "now give me the money and you won't get hurt." Smith handed over to him more than $1,000 in small bills. Stuffing them into a light tan satchel, the robber fled out the door.

Smith pushed the burglar alarm, a bell which rang loudly enough to alert a policeman who was patrolling the area. As the policeman hurried to the store, Smith rushed outside, but many people were on the city sidewalks and he couldn't spot the robber.

The policeman asked the manager, the store employees, and the customers who had remained, to describe the man.

"What did he look like?"

"What was he wearing?"

"How tall was he?"

"What color was his hair?"

Upon receiving as complete a picture of the robber as he could, he telephoned the nearest police station house. The radio dispatcher at the station house alerted police cars throughout the city to be on the lookout for a man in a blue coat carrying a light tan bag. The station house also notified the main police headquarters, which put in a call for a detective. The detective bureau called the policeman at the store to say that one of their men would be at the store the next morning. After taking the names of the witnesses, the policeman left, and the manager closed the store for the day.

The next morning, the detective interviewed Smith. He had received a report from headquarters that no similar robberies had been committed recently in the neighborhood.

"Do you normally have so much money in your store?" the detective asked the manager.

"Wednesday is pay day, and the money had just come into the store," Smith replied.

"Do most of the other businesses around here have pay days on Wednesday?"

"I can't really say," the manager answered. "But I think a lot of them pay their employees on Friday."

"Sounds like it may have been someone who knew something about the store or someone from the neighborhood, or both," the detective mused to himself. "Is there anything else you can remember about the holdup?" he asked aloud.

"Well, not really. The man came in waving his gun and said if nobody moved, nobody would get hurt. Then he said to me, 'All right, Smith, give me the money'."

"He called you by your *name?*"

"Yes, that's right!"

"Do you know of anyone with a grudge against you?"

"Well, I can think of a few people, maybe, but they wouldn't know about Wednesday being pay day."

"Then he must be connected with the store."

"No, he couldn't be," the manager said, "because all our employees were here."

"Well, someone who *used* to work for the store. Think."

THE SUSPECT

Smith then remembered Tom Mountebank, who had worked at the store two years before and who had been fired because he was caught taking money from the cash register.

"That might be the guy," the detective said. He looked up Mountebank's address in the telephone book, called headquarters to see what information the police had on the suspect, and went to Mountebank's home a few blocks away.

A person fitting the general description of the robber opened the door. "You Tom Mountebank?" the detective asked.

"Yes. Why? Who are you?"

"I'm a police detective." He showed Mountebank his badge. "Do you mind answering a few questions?"

"No. What's this all about? I haven't done anything." Mountebank seemed nervous.

"I didn't say you did. Did you ever work for the corner drug store a couple of blocks over?"

"Yes."

"Where were you yesterday afternoon?"

"Yesterday afternoon?"

"That's what I asked." Before Mountebank answered, the detective spotted a blue coat lying on a chair across the room.

"I was with a friend of mine. We were here all afternoon."

"That your coat?"

Mountebank turned to look at it. "Yeah, say what is this, anyway?"

"Nothing, just stick around town, Mountebank," the detective answered.

"Yeah, I'm not going anywhere."

THE WARRANT

The detective, on his return to the police station, called the friend with whom Mountebank said he had been during the previous afternoon. The friend said he hadn't seen Mountebank in six months. Everything pointed toward Mountebank's being the robber, so the detective went to the office of the district attorney ("D.A."), the chief criminal law enforcement officer in the city. One of the D.A.'s assistants, after hearing the evidence against Mountebank, wrote up a "warrant" (a document naming the person suspected of having committed a crime, and describing the suspicious facts), authorizing the arrest and a search of the suspect's apartment. The detective then took the warrant to the "magistrate" (judge) at the city courthouse to be formally "issued" (approved and signed). The magistrate was satisfied from the detective's testimony that sufficient grounds to suspect Mountebank existed, so he issued the warrant.

All this was needed because the Fourth Amendment to the United States Constitution states that no one can be arrested unless there is "probable cause" to suspect him of having committed the crime. The Fourth Amendment also directs the police to obtain a warrant before arresting a suspect unless there is not sufficient time to prevent his escape. It would have been unconstitutional to arrest a number of people at random and hope to pick the robber from the group.

The laws are even more strict in the case of a "citizen's arrest." If you see someone robbing a store, you are permitted to "arrest" him if you can, and turn him over to the police. However, if you are mistaken in believing that he was a thief, he can sue you. He cannot sue a policeman who makes the same mistake. For this reason, and because criminals are dangerous, it is better to wait for the police to make the arrest.

THE ARREST

The detective took the warrant from the magistrate and, with a policeman, drove to Mountebank's house and arrested him. While the policeman stood with Mountebank, the detective searched the rooms and found $1,000 in small bills hidden in the broiler of the stove.

"I want to inform you of your rights," the detective said to Mountebank. "You don't have to say anything, but anything you do say can be used as evidence against you at the trial. You are entitled to a lawyer if you want one."

"I don't need a lawyer and I've got nothing to say," Mountebank replied.

"Where'd you get this money?" the detective asked.

"I don't have the slightest idea where it came from," Mountebank said.

"Where's your gun?"

"I have no gun."

Meanwhile, the detective was searching for the missing gun.

"Let's go," he finally said, having been unsuccessful in his search. The three then rode off to the city jail.

THE CONFESSION

The Fifth Amendment to the Constitution declares that no person can be made to testify against himself. If the police, by using physical force, compel an accused man to confess that he committed a robbery (sometimes called the "third degree"), the judge at the trial must refuse to let the confession be admitted in evidence. He must hold a hearing before the jurors come into the courtroom, to determine whether the confession was coerced, if the issue is raised. (Confessions are not limited to verbal statements. In one case, the police pumped a man's stomach against his will to get some evidence he had swallowed. The Supreme Court ruled that the pumping was unconstitutional.)

At the police station, Mountebank was fingerprinted and "booked" (his name was entered in a special book, and the time he was brought in and the nature of the charges were noted). The police began questioning him, but still Mountebank denied knowing anything about the robbery or the money or the gun. After about two hours of questioning, Mountebank was taken to another part of the police station and put in a "lineup." Along with four other men, Mountebank stood against a wall, wearing the blue coat. Smith, the cashier-manager, and some of the shoppers had been asked to come to police headquarters to identify the suspect. All of them pointed to Mountebank as the person they had seen rob the store.

Mountebank and the policemen returned to the questioning room where for six more hours he was asked to explain where the money had come from and how he could deny having committed the robbery. Finally, after a total of eight hours of questioning, Mountebank confessed to the crime and signed a statement which the police had prepared.

THE PRELIMINARY HEARING

It was well into evening. Mountebank was put in jail for the night and the next morning brought before the magistrate for a "preliminary hearing." The magistrate advised him of his right to counsel, and this time Mountebank asked for a lawyer.

"Do you have money to retain your own counsel?" the magistrate asked.

"No, I don't have any money, period," Mountebank answered.

"We will continue (adjourn) the hearing for two days. I will appoint an attorney from the public defender's office," the magistrate said.

The judge was following the Sixth Amendment to the Constitution which guarantees the "right to counsel" in all criminal cases. In the Florida case of *Gideon v. Wainwright* in 1963 the Supreme Court said that the Amendment means an indigent (poor) defendant is entitled to a lawyer at state expense. In that case, Gideon, the defendant, could not afford a lawyer, and the judge refused to appoint one. Gideon tried to prove by himself that he was innocent, but he was convicted of stealing. From his jail cell, he wrote a letter to the U.S. Supreme Court, asking for a review of his case. The Supreme Court agreed, and appointed Abe Fortas (who was later appointed a Justice of the Supreme Court by President Johnson) to argue the case for Gideon. Following the argument, the Supreme Court ruled that the Sixth Amendment required Florida to hire a lawyer for Gideon. So a new Florida trial was ordered, and this time with a defense lawyer, Gideon was proven innocent.

[Note: originally, the Fourth, Fifth, Sixth, and other Amendments in the Bill of Rights applied only to the federal government. After the Civil War the Fourteenth Amendment was ratified (1868); it says that no *state* shall "deprive any person of life, liberty, or property without due process of law." In recent years, the Supreme Court has ruled that a state cannot legally do what the federal government cannot do under the original Bill of Rights, such as coerce a confession, because it will have violated the "due process clause" of the Fourteenth Amendment. In other words, the Bill of Rights is being made applicable to the states because of the Fourteenth Amendment.]

The criminal law is highly complicated and only a trained lawyer can defend someone properly. The magistrate in the Mountebank case called the probation officer to report on the accused's past record. Mountebank had been convicted of assault and battery with a dangerous weapon and received a suspended sentence and a two-year probation period; he had also been convicted of "petty larceny" (stealing a small sum) and received a six-month jail sentence.

Bail

"Bail is set at $10,000," the magistrate announced. The judge meant by this that if Mountebank were to pay that sum to the court to guarantee his appearance at the trial, he need not stay in jail during the two-day wait for the hearing. The bail money would be returned after the trial, but if the accused were to "jump bail" and not appear, the bail money would be forfeited to the state. Bail varies from $100 to $100,000, sometimes more. However, the amount of bail cannot be excessive—this is forbidden by the Eighth Amendment. The amount depends on how trustworthy the judge thinks the suspect is, and how serious the crime. When a defendant (like Mountebank) cannot raise the money for bail, he can sometimes borrow money from "bail bondsmen," professional bail money lenders. However, Mountebank could not afford the bondsman's interest rates, so he waited in jail.

The Public Defender

The day before the preliminary hearing, an attorney from the public defender's office came to interview Mountebank in his jail cell. The public defender is a state official, who, with a staff of lawyers, defends those whom the D.A. will prosecute. Only a minority of states now have public defenders, but it is thought their number will grow as more and more indigent defendants request counsel.

"I'm working for you, not for them," the attorney told Mountebank. "Tell me the whole true story. Did you do it?"

"No."

"Then how did the money get there?"

Mountebank was vague. "A friend gave it to me and asked me to hide it for him."

"Who was your friend?"

"Look, I'm not ratting on my friend," Mountebank said angrily.

"If you don't tell me who he is, you'll take the rap for this crime. You'll be sentenced to ten years or more."

"You're the lawyer. I'm not taking the rap for anyone. You get me off."

"How can I get you off when you won't tell me anything? What about an alibi? Where were you when that robbery happened?"

"I was in the park across town, just walking along."

"Were you with anyone?"

"No, just walking along by myself, not hurting anyone, just walking along."

So the conversation went for another hour, with the lawyer trying to uncover some facts to build up his side of the case for his distressed client.

The next day, when the preliminary hearing resumed, the magistrate presided and the district attorney first presented his evidence. The defendant (Mountebank), his attorney, the store manager, and the arresting policeman and detective were present. After questioning of all witnesses by both the district attorney and the public defender, the defendant was called to testify but he had "nothing to say." The magistrate found "probable cause" to hold Mountebank and "bound" him over to the "grand jury," which was to meet in two days.

THE GRAND JURY

The grand jury ordinarily consists of 23 jurors chosen from lists of registered voters in the community. They sit as a committee of ordinary citizens, who meet for the purpose of assessing once again whether there is probable cause to hold a suspect, and enough evidence against the person to justify holding a trial. The district attorney presided at this grand jury session and presented Mountebank's confession. He called on the arresting officers to make their statements, and questioned the store manager, who said that Mountebank looked like the robber and had worked at the store. The grand jury is a closed proceeding; the public is not welcome. Mountebank chose to testify on his own behalf, telling the jurors that he had no idea where the money came from and that he was innocent. The jury retired to deliberate; 15 minutes later it returned, a majority having agreed to hand down an "indictment" (formal charge) of armed robbery.

THE ARRAIGNMENT

The defendant was returned to jail to wait for his trial, set for three weeks later, which was the earliest opening on the "trial docket" or calendar. The Sixth Amendment declares that every criminal defendant is entitled to a "speedy and public trial." The day after the indictment, the defendant was "arraigned" before the magistrate. He stood in open court and heard the charge of armed robbery made against him in the indictment.

After the indictment was read, the judge asked, "How does the defendant plead?"

On his lawyer's coaching, Mountebank replied, "I plead not guilty, your Honor."

Had he entered a "plea" (answer to the charge) of guilty, no trial would have been necessary; he would have been sentenced by the judge. In minor criminal cases, the defendant can enter a plea of "*nolo contendere*" (no contest) which means that the defendant does not admit guilt, but is not willing to incur the expense of a trial and will pay the fine imposed on him by the judge.

Neither the public defender nor the district attorney stopped working on the case during the wait for trial. Two weeks before, they both were present at a "pre-trial hearing," presided over by the trial judge (a different judge than the magistrate who had been holding the hearings up until now). At the hearing the most important motion was made by Mountebank's attorney, who asked that the confession be excluded from the trial on the grounds that it was coerced. The judge, feeling that the evidence did not show that the confession had been coerced, denied the motion.

During the final week before trial, Mountebank's lawyer had finished his investigation and preparation. He had gone to the park to see whether he could find anyone who might have seen Mountebank, but was unsuccessful. He had talked to Mountebank's few friends. He had thoroughly researched the law of his case, reading up on armed robbery. He had discussed with Mountebank whether he should take the stand in his own defense. If Mountebank did take the stand, he would subject himself to cross-examination by the prosecutor who would certainly bring out his past criminal record. This would tend to "impeach" (discredit) his testimony. But if Mountebank decided not to take the stand, he would have no defense, and the jury might feel that he was trying to hide his guilt. (The jury would be specifically instructed against drawing such a conclusion. The law is well settled that the failure of the defendant to take the stand on his own behalf is not to be used against him. Nevertheless, the jury may draw the conclusion anyway, and the defendant must weigh the possibility.)

THE JURY

On the morning set for trial, the jury was picked. From a list of registered voters, 70 people had been summoned to the courthouse to participate in the "*voir dire*" (old French for "to tell the truth"), a proceeding to determine whether a person is a fit juror for a particular case (or to examine a witness's qualifications to make certain statements). With an official of the court presiding, an assistant district attorney and the defendant's attorney alternately questioned the prospective jurors.

"Do you have any knowledge of the facts of the case?"

"Do you know the defendant, Mountebank?"

"Do you have a financial interest in the store?"

"Do you know any store employees?"

"Are you related to any of the parties or their counsel?"

When one of the persons turned out to be a cousin of the store manager, Mountebank's attorney moved to have him excluded. The judge granted the motion and the cousin was barred from sitting on the Mountebank jury, although he might be picked for another jury chosen later that day. Finally, seven men and five women—12 in all—were chosen to try Tom Mountebank for robbery.

The jury was sworn in by a clerk of the court and the first juror chosen was named "foreman" (the juror who acts as a spokesman). Suddenly from a side door leading from his chambers, the judge entered the courtroom, wearing a long black garment, the traditional robe of a judge. Everyone—jury, lawyers, Mountebank, and the public—stood up until the judge sat down behind the high bench at one end of the courtroom. The stenographer, ready to write down everything that was said for the record, was at her special stenotype machine. The judge banged his gavel, and the court clerk announced, "The case of the State versus Thomas Mountebank." Then the trial began.

THE TRIAL

The district attorney and the attorney from the public defender's office each made an opening statement to the jury, outlining what they were going to prove during the course of the trial: the district attorney, that Mountebank was guilty of robbing the store of $1,000; Mountebank's attorney, that he was innocent.

In any trial, the plaintiff has the "burden of proof." Here, the state as prosecutor must prove *beyond a reasonable doubt* that Mountebank committed the robbery. If there is a reasonable doubt, no matter how slight, in the minds of the jurors, the defendant must be "acquitted" (found not guilty). This puts a very heavy burden on the prosecution. Thus, the principle "innocent until proven guilty" is carried out in practice.

Examination of the Witnesses

The district attorney stood up and called the state's first witness. It was Smith, the store manager.

He was "placed under oath" by a clerk: "Do you swear to tell the truth, the whole truth, and nothing but the truth?" (After taking this oath, a witness is legally obligated to be truthful. If he lies, he can be found guilty of perjury and sent to jail.)

The district attorney questioned the manager to bring out Smith's version of the story. "On what day did the robbery occur?"

"On Wednesday, July 23rd."

"How much money was taken?"

"About $1,000."

"How did you happen to have so much money in the store?"

"Wednesday is pay day."

"For how many years has it been pay day?"

"More than four years now."

"Was the defendant Mountebank ever employed by your store?"

"Yes."

"How long ago and for how long?"

"Two years ago for about six months, I think."

"So then the defendant must have known that Wednesday was your pay day?"

Mountebank's lawyer jumped up. "Objection, your Honor, the question calls for a conclusion on the part of the witness."

"Objection sustained," the judge said. "The jury will disregard the question."

A witness is supposed to testify only to what he saw or heard, and only the jury may draw inferences or conclusions as to the actual facts. Of course, the inference that Mountebank did know that Wednesday was pay day had now been suggested to the jury, even though the question was not answered.

"Why did you fire the defendant?" the district attorney asked, as he continued his questioning.

The judge smiled. "That's another question defense counsel should object to," he thought to himself.

Sure enough, Mountebank's lawyer jumped up and thundered once again, "Objection, your Honor, counsel is leading the witness."

Once again the judge sustained the objection and told the jury to disregard the question. There is a rule which forbids a lawyer to ask his own witness a "leading question" (one which suggests to the witness the answer desired). In this case it had never been established that the store had "fired" Mountebank; he might have left the store's employ for any number of reasons. By asking why the store had fired Mountebank, the district attorney was suggesting to the witness and to the jury that Mountebank had been fired. The district attorney restated the question:

"Was the defendant discharged from his job?"

"Yes, he was."

"Please tell us the reason."

"He took money from the cash register."

When the district attorney was through questioning Smith, it was Mountebank's lawyer's turn to conduct a "cross-examination" of the witness. He asked questions aimed at showing that Smith's testimony did not necessarily prove that Mountebank had robbed the store.

"Do you wear a store uniform or jacket?" Mountebank's lawyer asked the manager.

"Yes, a jacket."

"Would you tell the jury what it says right over the pocket?"

"It has my name on it, Smith," he answered.

"Were you wearing this jacket when the store was robbed?"

"Yes."

"Did it have your name on it at that time?"

"Yes."

A few more questions along this line told the jury that one reason the robber may have called Smith by his name was because he had read it on the uniform, not because he had known the manager.

"Were you the manager of the store when the defendant was discharged?"

"I was."

"Did you catch him taking money?"

"No, I did not."

"Then you don't know that he took money."

"The store owner told me he suspected Mountebank, and ordered me to fire him."

"Then you don't yourself know if the defendant took money or not. You only heard someone say so."

"I guess that's right."

The defense attorney was driving at what is called "hearsay evidence" which is not admissible evidence if the person a witness quotes is not in court to face cross-examination. In this instance, the defense attorney brought out the hearsay and discredited the witness to some extent.

When the cross-examination of the manager was finished, the district attorney called his next witness, the policeman who had fingerprinted Mountebank when he was booked. The policeman testified that he had examined Mountebank's fingerprints and compared them with fingerprints found on one of the dollar bills—and that they were the same. Notice that this testimony involves drawing a conclusion. When the defense attorney objected, the judge overruled the objection. Conclusions drawn by "experts" are oftentimes "put in evidence." This is allowed because jurors would not be expected to know what to look for in deciding whether fingerprints were the same. The district attorney felt that the jury would believe his expert in the absence of evidence to the contrary (such as conflicting testimony from another expert witness), and he thought the testimony of the policeman gave weight to the state's case. The defense attorney, on the other hand, did not cross-examine the witness, because he might bring out facts about gathering fingerprints which the D.A. might elaborate on later in "redirect examination" (a second questioning of the witness by the friendly party's attorney). Since he did not want to emphasize the point, he allowed it to pass.

The judge then recessed the court an hour for lunch. When trial resumed, the detective testified about the arrest, how he found in Mountebank's home the blue coat and tan bag which the manager had described, and stated that

Mountebank had confessed to the robbery. At this point the district attorney asked leave of the court to read the confession to the jury.

"Objection," Mountebank's lawyer said. "The confession was involuntary, a result of coercion, and should be struck from the testimony."

"Objection overruled. You may proceed," the judge said to the district attorney.

"I ask that my objection be noted for the record," Mountebank's lawyer said. The judge agreed. This means that if Mountebank should be convicted and should decide to appeal, one ground for reversal would be the judge's alleged error in allowing the confession.

After the district attorney read the confession, Mountebank's lawyer cross-examined the detective.

"Did you find the gun?"

"Is it true that you questioned the defendant for eight hours?"

"Don't you think that after denying something 100 times anybody would agree to sign a statement just to get you to stop asking questions?"

The defense attorney asked these questions to show under what circumstances the confession was obtained. During cross-examination, the lawyer always faces a "hostile witness," one who has just testified on behalf of the other party. So the cross-examiner is allowed to ask what might be "leading questions" in order by skillful questioning to guide the witness into giving an answer which conflicts with statements he has already made or to bring out facts which cast doubt on the testimony the witness gave during "direct examination" (questioning by the friendly party's attorney). If the cross-examiner succeeds in this strategy, the jury will usually decide that the witness is unreliable; even worse, the witness may have hurt the side for which he was testifying.

The Case for the Defendant

When the cross-examination ended, the state "rested" its case. It was now the defendant's turn to present his case. By the evidence his attorney introduced, he hoped to throw enough doubt into the jurors' minds to necessitate their bringing back a verdict of not guilty. Mountebank was his own and only witness; he denied committing the robbery; he denied owning a gun; he denied knowing how the money got into the broiler of his stove. After a short while, the defense also rested its case.

In his cross-examination, the district attorney brought out and emphasized

Mountebank's criminal record. He also questioned Mountebank at length on the money that had been found in his possession.

The Summing Up

Then Mountebank's lawyer addressed the jury. Speaking quietly, he "summed up" the defendant's side of the case. He discussed the defendant's impoverished early life, which had caused him to attempt to steal a few years earlier. He cautioned the jury against inferring from the defendant's history that Mountebank had robbed the store. The attorney advised the jury not to pay any attention to the confession, since it was "obviously coerced." Finally, because so many aspects of the case remained unexplained, especially the fact that the gun had never been found, he urged the jury to find reasonable doubt of Mountebank's guilt and to acquit him.

Following defense counsel, the district attorney rose to give his summation. The evidence all pointed "the finger of guilt" directly at Mountebank; his failure to explain how the money got to his room, plus the confession itself, established his guilt. He urged the jury to find Mountebank guilty so that he could be locked up and the public protected from such a dangerous person.

The Role of the Judge

When the lawyers finished their summations, the judge took the central stage. Up until now the judge's role had been mainly that of an umpire: he had made sure that no improper questions were asked or answered and he had kept order in the courtroom. But in giving his "instructions" to the jury, the judge played perhaps the most crucial part in the trial.

The judge must explain the *law* to the jury. It is not for the jurors to decide the law; their sole responsibility is to decide from all the conflicting testimony what the facts are and to apply the *facts* to the judge's explanation of the law to reach a verdict. The opposing attorneys may make suggestions as to what the instructions should be, but only the judge has the power to say what the law is. Should the judge fail to give an instruction which one of the lawyers recommended, that lawyer can later urge an appellate court to reverse the trial judge on the grounds that the judge made an error. The judge must therefore be careful to word his instructions precisely within the bounds of the law. Mountebank's judge in fact recessed the court for one hour to receive suggested instructions and to look up a point of law himself.

A jury, under our laws, decides what the facts are because it was long ago felt that "twelve heads are better than one." The jury is supposed to know nothing about the case initially, and to hear only the testimony which the judge thinks they should hear, according to the law.

In the present case, once the judge returned, he instructed the jury as follows:

"Ladies and gentlemen of the jury, you have heard all the testimony and it is now your duty to bring back a verdict. Under the law of this state, robbery is a felonious taking of personal property in the possession of another, from his person or immediate presence, and against his will, accomplished by means of force or fear. Where a person, either with violence or with threats of injury, and putting the person robbed in fear, takes and carries away a thing which is on the body, or in the immediate presence of the person from whom it is taken, under such circumstances that, in the absence of violence or threats, the act committed would be a theft, then he has committed a robbery.

"If you unanimously find beyond a reasonable doubt that the defendant, Thomas Mountebank, did take the money alleged to have been found in his house from the store, accomplishing his taking by means of force or fear, against the will of the store manager, Smith, then you must bring back a verdict of guilty.

"If you find that the defendant committed violent acts or threats, with the aid of a gun, during the commission of the robbery, you must find him guilty of armed robbery.

"If, on the other hand, you find a reasonable doubt exists as to whether the defendant was the person in question or as to whether he took the money by force or by fear, or as to whether he took it against the will of the store manager, then you are to return a verdict of not guilty.

"If you decide that the confession was involuntarily given, that is, not given of the defendant's own free will, but was coerced from him, then you are to disregard the confession when you deliberate as to defendant's guilt or innocence.

"The bulk of the evidence you heard was from the state's witnesses. You should consider the credibility of the witnesses and not just the number.

"It is your duty to decide what the facts of the case are and to decide, according to the rules of law which I have just explained, whether the defendant is innocent or guilty. You may not agree with the law, but it *is* the law and you must follow it."

Does that sound confusing? Very often the judge's instructions *are* confusing to a jury. Members of the jury may ask the judge for more instructions—in effect, an explanation of his explanation of the law. But the jury must pay close attention to the judge. Many laws are very complicated and explanation in simple language isn't always possible. Various groups of lawyers and judges in many states are now in the process of working out simplifications of wording which all juries will understand.

The Verdict

The 12 jurors then retired to the jury room, a small room off the public courtroom. For three hours they deliberated until they finally all agreed. The foreman wrote a note in the jury room which the "bailiff" (a court official responsible for the jury's privacy) took to the judge. Upon reading that the jury had reached its verdict, the judge summoned the jurors back to the courtroom in the presence of the defendant, his counsel, the district attorney, and the public.

The judge asked Mountebank to stand. "Has the jury reached its verdict?" the judge asked the foreman.

"We have, your Honor," the foreman replied.

The judge asked the jury whether everyone was in agreement. The jurors nodded their heads, and the judge, hearing nothing to the contrary, asked for the verdict.

"We find the defendant Thomas Mountebank guilty of armed robbery."

The judge adjourned the trial, announcing that he would sentence the defendant in one week's time. Then the probation officer investigated Mountebank's history and background, his past record and his present circumstances, and made a report and recommendation to the judge.

At the sentencing, the judge declared: "The law directs me to sentence you to from 5 to 20 years in the state penitentiary. On the basis of your past record, the gravity of your crime, and the report as to your character, I sentence you to 15 years."

As Mountebank was removed to the city jail pending his transfer to the state prison, his attorney notified the judge that he would appeal the case. Had Mountebank been acquitted he would have been freed, never to be tried for that crime again; the state could not have appealed. This is the right against "double jeopardy" guaranteed by the Fifth Amendment.

Guards at the state penitentiary greeted Mountebank the day he began the life of a "convict." His lawyer was far away, searching through a pile of law books, beginning his research for the first of what turned out to be many appeals. During the next months, Mountebank's lawyer argued two state appeals and one "rehearing" before the state supreme court. He argued that evidence was unlawfully admitted, that the judge incorrectly instructed the jury on the law, that the prosecutor was allowed to ask improper questions, and that the confession was coerced and should not have been admitted in evidence. But all the appeals were rejected and the judgment of the lower court was affirmed: Mountebank was guilty and must remain in jail. That was not the end, however.

Further Recourse

The very day he lost his last appeal in state supreme court, Mountebank's lawyer filed a petition for a "writ" (order) of "*habeas corpus*" in the federal district court. *Habeas corpus* (meaning roughly "you have the body") is an order to direct the jailer to produce the person in court unless the imprisonment can be justified. Because applying for *habeas corpus* is a federal constitutional right, it can be sought in federal courts for state crimes. Mountebank's lawyer claimed that because the police questioned Mountebank for eight hours, the confession was necessarily coerced and that Mountebank was therefore deprived of his constitutional right under the Fifth Amendment not to incriminate himself. The lawyer asked for a new trial and a "change of venue" (change in location of the court for trial). Mountebank wanted his new trial in a different county, where jurors could be found who would not have read about the trial and the appeals and would not, therefore, be biased.

The federal district court denied the writ of *habeas corpus*, as did the federal circuit court of appeals, to which the lower court's decision was appealed.

So Mountebank's lawyer prepared for an appeal to the United States Supreme Court. It was now more than two years after Mountebank had been sentenced. The Supreme Court heard the argument and this time Mountebank won: the court reasoned that eight hours is too long a time for the police to continue questioning. If the police realize they cannot use such confessions they will have no reason to try to get them. In order to make sure the police do not deprive a suspect of his Fifth Amendment rights, the Court decided not to allow the confession (the product of the deprivation) to be used in evidence. So a new trial had to be held, with a change of venue.

But, even without the confession, the verdict again went against Mountebank. Again his lawyer appealed the decision in the state courts and again he lost. He instituted a new *habeas corpus* petition in federal district court and lost. The federal appeals court affirmed the decision. This time, four years after the first sentencing, the Supreme Court refused to review the decision of the federal appellate court. Mountebank was legally in jail, and he would have to continue serving his term.

It may seem that the criminal legal process is long, elaborate and cumbersome. Some people have so criticized it, and have suggested many reforms. But the very seriousness of a criminal conviction requires great precautions. Innocent people must be protected by the law and the courts; they must not be held on mere suspicion. The rights and dignity of guilty defendants not yet convicted must be upheld.

To be tried and convicted of a crime is perhaps the most serious thing that can happen to a man in our society, and it is necessary that the utmost caution and care be used throughout the process of criminal law.

Part III: A Spectrum of Cases

The cases we have just looked at illustrate the two basic branches of the common law—the "civil" side and the "criminal" side.

The fundamental aim of civil law is to compensate someone when another wrongfully injures him or his property or deprives him of something to which he is entitled either by ordering financial compensation for a wrong or by ordering a defendant to take the necessary steps to repair or stop the injury. The civil law serves to settle a number of kinds of disagreements among individuals. Within this broad category of the civil common law there are two main branches. The first is "the law of torts."

TORTS

A tort is any wrongful injury. The person who commits the tort (called the "tortfeasor") may have intention to do the act, or he may simply have been careless. In some cases, a person may commit a tort without wanting to cause injury, and may even have taken elaborate precautions to prevent it.

Intentional Torts

There are quite a variety of intentional torts. If someone intends to hit you, comes up swinging his fist, but misses, he has committed an "assault." If he actually hits you, he has committed "assault and battery." This is also a crime, so that two lawsuits are possible. A civil suit can be brought to recover for injuries; the state can bring a criminal suit, to prosecute the assailant for breaking the law. But these are two separate suits, and either one is possible without the other. If a person wants to "recover" for his injuries by means of legal processes, he must bring the civil suit himself.

Suppose someone kidnaps you (a crime) and keeps you imprisoned in a cellar; suppose he knows you're in a room, looks the door, and won't let you out, even though you ask him to. He has committed the tort of "false imprisonment."

Assume now that someone takes your property; you can sue for recovery of the value of the property. Or suppose someone walks onto your private land and damages your trees or house—this is known as "trespass" and you can recover "damages" in court. (The money judgment ordered as compensation in a civil suit is called "damages," a legal shorthand used to signify that the money is being awarded because the defendant caused damage.)

Negligence Torts

Many times torts are committed even though the tortfeasor has not the slightest intention of causing harm. One of the very oldest principles of the common law holds that everyone owes a certain "duty of care" to his fellow man. If you don't watch what you're doing, if you're careless or negligent, you may have to answer for it in court.

Every accident is not necessarily a tort, however. Underlying the theory of negligence (and indeed, underlying much of law itself) is the idea of "reasonableness." If a person has done what a reasonable person in his situation would not have done, he has committed a tort. (It is up to each jury to decide, as part of its finding of fact, what a reasonable man would have done in the circumstances of the case. Against this standard are measured the actions of the defendant.) What is reasonable depends not only on what was done, but also on who the defendant is. If a doctor is being sued for negligence, he will be held to a higher "standard of care" than a nurse. In short, reasonableness should be determined from *all* the circumstances of the given case.

In most negligence cases, if the defendant was negligent, he will lose, unless the plaintiff was negligent also. This is the doctrine of "contributory negligence." Had the plaintiff not contributed his own carelessness, the accident would never have happened. Sometimes this doctrine can lead to harsh results, and it is not always used. It is not used in cases in which the defendant is being sued for an intentional tort, such as assault and battery. The fact that the plaintiff could have ducked his head makes no difference. The defendant will lose if he intended to harm the plaintiff, whether or not the plaintiff was careless in letting him.

Strict Liability

In some injury cases, the court will hold the defendant liable for damages even though he was not at fault. Suppose a drug manufacturer sells a pill which makes you ill. Even though he did not intend his pill to cause sickness, and even though he used every possible test before he marketed it to discover whether it would make people sick (and all the tests indicated that the pill was safe) he will nevertheless be held responsible under the doctrine of "strict liability."

Morally, it was not the manufacturer's fault that illness resulted, of course. Nevertheless, it was his fault in a sense, because no illness would have been caused had he not put the pill on the market. True, no one has to buy the pill, but the law would provide little protection if the only way to prevent possible bad.effects when you need a pill, is not to use it.

A manufacturer, in figuring his costs on a product that can cause injury, adds a percentage for "liability insurance." Sometimes he takes out a policy with an insurance company.

Torts Against Intangibles

Some acts do not cause injury to the body or to physical property, but they may cause serious damage nonetheless. For instance, if someone tells a number of his friends that Dr. Johnson has performed many bad operations, Dr. Johnson will suffer a loss in reputation and many patients may stop visiting him. If what is said, written, or broadcast is false, Dr. Johnson can bring a tort action for "slander" or "libel."

Another tort caused by an interference with an intangible is "misrepresentation." If you buy a painting because the dealer tells you it is an original work, yet he knows, or has reason to think, that it is not, you can sue for the return of your money. He has misrepresented to you the item you are buying.

There are a number of other torts of this kind. Suppose someone deliberately humiliates you before a number of people. You can bring an action for "mental suffering." Suppose someone sues you just to cause trouble, when he knows he cannot possibly win. You can turn around and sue him for the tort of "malicious prosecution." Or, suppose someone without your permission publishes a personal letter you have written him. You can sue for "invasion of privacy."

CONTRACTS

The second broad branch of civil common law is called "contracts." The Case of the Missing House was of course a case in contract law. Legally speaking, a contract is an agreement ("a meeting of the minds") between people, or groups, or companies, or governments, or any combination of these.

In the law of torts, courts impose standards on people in their dealings with others. You have to be careful when you drive a car because the courts through the years have declared that you owe a duty of care to other drivers and to pedestrians. But in the law of contracts, private parties create legal relationships themselves. A court will almost never make you carry out a contract which you did not make. The duty to fulfill your part of the bargain arises only because you yourself have made a contract. In a sense, then, you "make your own law" when you enter into a contract.

A tort suit compensates the wronged party for his injury. A contract suit often does more. The law of contracts allows the plaintiff to recover his "expectancy"—what he expected to get out ot the contract.

This does not mean, however, that the plaintiff will always get the exact thing for which he contracted. If he has a contract to buy a car and the dealer has sold the car to someone else, he cannot get *that* car. But he can get one like it. Or he will be able to collect money damages equal to the worth of the car he was supposed to get.

Sometimes the court will order the defendant to give the plaintiff the very object. Usually this will happen when the contract concerns unique items, such as "real estate" (land and buildings), rare paintings, or objects of sentimental value. The court will order the seller to hand over a deed to the item in exchange for the buyer's money. This is "specific performance," because the defendant must perform his side of the bargain exactly as the contract is written. The court will not let him breach the contract.

Oral Contracts and Written Contracts

You may have heard someone say, "Oh, that contract was no good; it wasn't written down." If you broke a contract on that advice you would probably find yourself in trouble. Many oral contracts are just as binding and enforceable as written ones. In general, three kinds of contracts must be written down and signed in order for a court to uphold them:

(1) those for the sale of certain goods above certain prices,

(2) those for the sale of real estate, and

(3) those for services which are expected to continue for more than a year after the contract is made. The requirement that these kinds of contracts be in writing dates back to 1677 when the British Parliament passed the "Statute of Frauds." The purpose of the Statute was to prevent a party to a suit from fooling a jury by claiming that he had made a contract when he really had not. The Statute of Frauds has been adopted in some form by all states.

Most other kinds of contracts are just as good whether they are in writing or were merely agreed to orally. Of course, it is always better to have a written contract, because the problem of *proof* is easier. The written piece of paper is good evidence that a contract was made; often there are no witnesses to hear an oral contract, and the plaintiff may therefore find it impossible to prove his case to a jury.

Bilateral and Unilateral Contracts

Suppose I promise to give someone a car. Is that a contract? Even if it is a written promise, it is not a contract, since a binding contract requires *mutual* promises or acts. Had he promised me $200 in return, we would have a binding contract. The thing given in return is known in the law of contracts as the "consideration."

The consideration does not always have to be another promise. It can be an act. For instance, if I say, "I'll give you $5 if you'll wash my car," you don't have to *promise* me you'll wash my car in order to get the money. You have to *wash* the car. By performing the act you become entitled to the consideration of $5.

Contracts that depend upon mutual *promises* are called "bilateral" contracts because they are binding on both parties from the moment they are made. But a contract which depends upon a promise and an act is called a "unilateral" contract because it is only binding on one side. You do not have to do the act, but if you do, I am under a legal obligation to keep my promise.

Of course, I can always "revoke" (take back) my offer or promise before you actually do your part. Suppose, however, just before you finish washing the car I tell you the "deal is off." Most courts will make me keep my promise. The doctrine of "substantial performance" holds that it would be unfair to make you do *most* of what I wanted without my having to keep my part of the bargain.

The law of contracts can get highly complicated. Many lawyers spend their entire working days writing contracts, going over the "fine print" to make sure that their clients' interests are protected. When the terms of a contract are disputed in court the judge must decide what the terms mean. The clearer and less ambiguous the terms are from the start, the less chance there will be that a dispute will end in court, and the less chance that the judge will fix a meaning contrary to what a party originally intended.

We live in a commercial world. Billions of dollars worth of business is conducted every year. If there were no way to enforce promises, or determine their meaning, our businesses, industries, and government would come to a halt. Without a law of contracts, our entire civilization, as we know it, would collapse.

CRIMINAL LAW

Criminal law does not compensate the victims of crime. It serves "to bring criminals to justice," to regulate the affairs of society by declaring what is acceptable behavior and what is not. Because crimes are acts which the people, through their state legislatures and Congress, have decided are so dangerous as to require punishment, it is important that everyone know what kinds of acts are illegal or "against the law." Since most people know what kinds of behavior are not condoned by law and know that those acts will not go unpunished, the criminal law fulfills a primary purpose: "deterrence." If a person knows he will be severely punished for murdering, he will weigh the risks of being captured against the reasons he has for killing, and decide that murder isn't worth the price. Deterrence only functions in practice if laws are known and enforced.

To facilitate the regulation of public behavior, some crimes are declared by the legislatures and Congress to be more serious than others. The most serious are "felonies": these include murder, theft, kidnapping, arson, sale of narcotics. Heavy fines and long jail terms are attached to the commission of these crimes. Less serious crimes, such as speeding and breach of the peace are "misdemeanors," which carry small fines or short jail sentences. What is a felony in one state may be a misdemeanor in another.

In our cases, did you notice the similarities and differences between civil and criminal proceedings? In civil proceedings, the police are not usually involved at all, or at most are involved only indirectly. In civil cases the plaintiff is usually a private party. (However, if someone breaks a contract with the government, the state may bring a civil suit as plaintiff.) In criminal cases, the plaintiff is always the state or a governmental agent. The lawyer for the plaintiff in a criminal trial is called the prosecutor, and he may be the district attorney or his assistant. A criminal trial is conducted on behalf of the people of the state; the prosecutor and other lawyers on the government's side are paid by the taxpayers.

There are no grand juries in civil cases, but the United States Government under the Fifth Amendment must use grand juries in federal criminal cases. Many states, though not required to do so by the U.S. Constitution, are required by their own constitution or laws to use grand juries in criminal cases.

In both civil and criminal cases, complaints and answers are necessary. (The complaint in a criminal trial is the "indictment" and the answer is the "plea." In states which do not use grand juries the district attorney files an "information" against the defendant. This serves the same purpose as the indictment; it charges the defendant with a specific crime.)

In both civil and criminal cases the plaintiff bears the burden of proof. But in civil cases the plaintiff must prove merely that it is *more probable than not* that the defendant did what the plaintiff claims. The state in a criminal case must prove its case *beyond a reasonable doubt.*

In a civil suit the plaintiff is never sure he can collect his *judgment,* for the defendant may have no money to pay. A *sentence* in a criminal suit, on the other hand, will almost always be enforced. The prisoner is under policy custody and can be put in jail. (If the sentence is a fine and he cannot pay, he is usually sent to jail instead. A defendant in civil suits is not put in jail merely for inability to pay.)

Payment in a civil suit is to compensate the injured victim, but the sentence in a criminal suit is not compensation. If the guilty party is fined, the money goes to the state.

The line between criminal behavior and behavior which is merely wrongful under the civil common law is sometimes very thin.

What is criminal behavior? It is too simple to say, as some do, that it is anti-social behavior. To break a contract might be considered anti-social, for instance, since a large part of society depends on promises being kept, but to break a contract is not considered criminal. Fundamentally, crimes are those acts from which society feels it needs more protection than the civil law gives.

Since we live in a free society, the law does not regulate every aspect of our behavior. We are free to make countless kinds of contracts. If a contract is broken, the state does not act unless the aggrieved person brings suit. If I break a contract with you and you decide not to sue me, that is your concern and no one else's. But if someone steals from you and you do not care, society *does* care. The state puts the thief behind bars, even if *you* don't care what happens to the thief after your property is returned to you.

In the final analysis, criminal behavior is what the legislature says it is, subject to a few constitutional restrictions. The legislature cannot make it a criminal offense to criticize public officials, for instance. The First Amendment protects freedom of speech and prohibits such a law. Article I of the Constitution is more explicit in barring two general kinds of laws: the "bill of attainder" and the "*ex post facto* law." ("*Ex post facto*" is Latin for "after the deed.")

In England, the Parliament used to pass laws declaring various people guilty of crimes. No trials were allowed. Such laws were called "bills of attainder." Parliament also used to pass "*ex post facto* laws" which said that an act which someone did before the law was passed was illegal, even though when he did it the act was not illegal at all.

Because these two kinds of laws were so unjust the original Constitution declared that they can never be used in the United States. We are still protected in this regard today. In June, 1965, the Supreme Court struck down as unconstitutional a federal law which stripped a West Coast labor union officer of his job and sent him to jail because of his political affiliations. This, the Court said, was a bill of attainder, and unconstitutional.

Statutes enacted by legislatures to change the civil law can, however, have "retroactive" effects. To draw a line between permissible retroactive statutes and unconstitutional *ex post facto* laws is extremely difficult.

Finally, one very important difference between civil and criminal law is with respect to the judge's power to make law. During the past decade, for instance, the law of torts has been undergoing a revolution. The doctrine of strict liability has been constantly expanded to take account of many kinds of dangerous and hazardous activities. Courts are increasingly overturning the doctrine of "charitable immunity" which formerly held that institutions such as hospitals were not liable for negligent acts which their staffs committed. It was thought that a charity which exists for the benefit of everyone should not have to pay out huge sums in damage suits. But it is gradually being realized that it is even more unfair to cause great injury to a patient and not reimburse him at all. The tort of "invasion of privacy" is constantly being extended by judges to fit new situations; a century ago there was no such tort at all.

But judges in the United States are constitutionally forbidden from extending the criminal law in the same way. A person can be indicted for a crime only if a statute passed by a state legislature or by Congress has specifically declared his alleged behavior to be criminal. Of course, judges still have full power to interpret the meaning of the criminal statutes, just as they can interpret the law in a civil case.

STATUTORY SUITS

Court suits are not limited to civil common law or criminal cases. Many "statutory proceedings" can be brought to the courts: Suits brought to recover money unreasonably charged by "common carriers," such as railroads; suits instituted to challenge the actions of corporations; suits to secure divorces; suits to recover from a union which breached its duty of "fair representation" of its members, or from a company which unlawfully refused to bargain with the union—all are suits brought because someone claims a right conferred on him by a statute. Many of these legal actions could not be brought "at common law" (prior to the enactment of the statutes). Sometimes the right claimed under a statute will not be upheld by a court unless a public agency has acted first. The National Labor Relations Board, for instance, must first determine whether an employer is guilty of an "unfair labor practice" before its order will be enforced by a court.

REMEDIES

"Remedies" are the crux of justice: if a person does not get the proper remedy, injustice has been done. Because getting the proper remedy is so crucial to any party to a lawsuit, courts are usually extremely flexible in making sure that the remedies fit the circumstances and extent of the injury. Over the years the scope of remedies has widened greatly. In the early history of our courts, the judges granted only very narrow relief, consisting of a few specifically named remedies, and these have today been expanding in scope. Some of these are briefly outlined below—they are illustrative of the variety of ways courts deal with situations people get into. The list is by no means complete. You should read for flavor, not to memorize.

Money Damages

The usual civil remedy is the "money judgment" or "damages." The amount can be flexibly calculated to try to compensate for harm. Often the calculation is difficult. How much is a leg worth? or a loved one? or a reputation? Is it fair for one jury to give $10,000 for physical injuries and another to give $50,000 for the same injuries? Disparities like this can happen. The judge has some power in lowering the amount of a judgment if he thinks it excessive, but he seldom, if ever, awards more than the jury does. An injured party who did not get as much as he hoped has difficulty in appealing for more. The problem is, of course, that money is an inadequate remedy for many injuries. Money does not stop pain or bring people back to life.

Injunction

Suppose your neighbor runs a buzz saw, making loud noises every night so that you cannot sleep. You can go to court and ask for an "injunction" (a court order) against him. If, after the trial, the judge agrees that your neighbor is unreasonable in making the noises (creating a "nuisance"), he will issue an injunction directing him to stop. Your neighbor is said to be "enjoined" from making the noises.

Temporary Restraining Order

If your neighbor likes to play with dynamite, you can get an even more drastic remedy. You can go to court and explain that unless the neighbor is stopped, your house may be destroyed. Without even listening to the neighbor's side of the story, the judge may issue a "temporary restraining order" (or "temporary injunction")—your neighbor must stop at once. If the judge still agrees with you after the trial, the restraining order will be changed to a "permanent injunction," forever forbidding your neighbor to use his dynamite and probably commanding him to remove it from his property altogether. If, however, the judge decides that the dynamite would not have hurt your house because it was going to be used in a small amount two miles away, you may have to pay your neighbor for whatever damages you caused him by delaying his work.

Specific Performance

As we have already seen, courts will sometimes direct the person who has breached a contract to do exactly what the contract called for. Like an injunction, specific performance will be granted only when a damage remedy would not be adequate, or when it involves unique objects.

Reformation

If something other than what is actually agreed to is mistakenly put in a written contract, a judge can order the contract "reformed" (rewritten correctly).

Rescission

If a person induces you to contract with him by misrepresenting what he will do or sell (the tort of "misrepresentation"), a judge can order the contract "rescinded" (made null and void).

Restitution

Suppose someone breaches a contract with you and refuses to give you back the money you paid him. You can recover the money by bringing an action for "restitution."

Garnishment

Suppose the defendant has lost a damage action and is ordered to pay to the plaintiff a sum which he does not have and cannot obtain. If the defendant has a job, his wages can be "garnisheed." This means his employer is placed under a legal obligation to deduct a small percentage of the defendant's salary from each paycheck and pay it to the court officer, who will pay it to the plaintiff. The amount that can be garnisheed is usually, although not always, controlled by state statute.

Attachment

If the losing defendant has no money but does have some property, the plaintiff can bring suit to have it "attached" (legally taken) by the court and sold by the sheriff at a public auction. The proceeds from the sale would be given to the plaintiff to "satisfy" the judgment; the remainder would be paid over to the defendant.

Civil Contempt

If, because of the defendant's willful action, none of the remedies bring relief to the plaintiff, the court can apply a "sanction" against the defendant by holding him "in contempt of court" (guilty of disobeying a court order) and can put him in jail until he agrees that if freed he will comply with the court's order. The defendant is often said "to carry the keys to freedom in his pocket" in civil contempt cases, since he has not committed a crime and the court must free him as soon as he agrees to co-operate.

SANCTIONS

Because the criminal law does not provide compensation for the victims of crime, civil law remedies are not sufficient under the criminal law. Rather, "sanctions" are placed throughout the criminal law process on criminals and potential criminals in order to deter law-offenders, to protect the public, to punish the guilty, and to "rehabilitate" (reform) the law-breaker so that he can play a useful role in society.

Fines

The most widespread sanction in the criminal law is the "fine," a money payment to the state ordered by the court when the defendant is convicted of a violation. Fines are imposed for infractions of the traffic laws (such as a $15 ticket for speeding) and for some of the worst felonies (such as a $10,000 fine for robbery).

Jail

If a fine hurts a defendant because he must pay for his crime with his property, prison hurts the convicted criminal more, because he must pay for his crime with his liberty. Jail sentences run anywhere from one night in the city jail to life imprisonment in a state or federal prison. The jail sentence serves many purposes: it protects society by putting dangerous criminals in prison; it deters would-be criminals by setting an example; it helps reform the criminal because he may be taught a useful trade in prison; and it punishes him for having broken the law. That, at least, is the idea; as we shall see later, there is serious question how well the jail sentence measures up to these ideals.

Capital Punishment

For many hundreds of years, "capital punishment" (death) was the penalty for almost all crimes in England. Many people were put to death on the flimsiest of evidence. The punishment was so harsh and so ill-suited to certain crimes that some judges refused to convict the defendants being tried. The deterrent effect of capital punishment in those years was perhaps not great. Capital punishment was recently prohibited in England, and a growing number of states in America are legislating it out of existence. But it still exists in some states as the penalty for murder, kidnapping, arson, rape, robbery, treason, and train-wrecking.

Many states provide different punishments for murder. The more serious the killing, the harsher is the sentence. A first-degree murderer—one who "premeditates" (plans out his crime deliberately in advance), or one who even accidentally kills someone during the commission of a felony—will be sentenced to death or life imprisonment. Unjustified killings can be unpremeditated or accidental, but are still considered crimes and are classified as second- or third-degree murder and manslaughter. Lesser sentences are provided.

Corporal Punishment

In all but a very few states, perhaps only one or two, "corporal punishment" (physical beating, such as flogging or whipping) is illegal. When the law was young, corporal punishment was widely used; this use extended into the 19th century in America. However, it has gradually died out.

The Eighth Amendment to the Constitution prohibits "cruel and unusual punishments." If a state legislature tried to make the penalty for speeding (or another crime considered minor) either death or some type of physical beating, the Supreme Court might rule such a punishment unconstitutional.

Parole

Most statutes setting the length of jail terms include a provision for "parole," a suspension of part of the sentence for good behavior. Conditions can be imposed on the paroled convict; if he does not live up to the conditions, such as remaining in a certain city, or working at a certain job, or reporting at regular intervals to the parole officer, he can be returned to jail for the remainder of his term.

Probation

Sometimes a convicted defendant may be placed on "probation" by the judge rather than sent to jail. Probation is similar to parole in that the person must obey the terms and conditions of the probation and must usually report to a probation officer.

Suspended Sentence

When a person is not sent to jail, but placed on probation, his sentence is said to be "suspended." A person receiving a suspended sentence is often put on probation, but the judge may simply let him go. The only sanction then is the shame of having been convicted as a criminal. The conviction stands and the defendant may lose certain rights (such as the right to run for public office).

Criminal Contempt

Normally no one but the Executive Branch of the government can initiate criminal proceedings in the courts. But sometimes, when a party to a suit acts in disrespect of the court, or interferes with the court's administration of justice, the court will initiate on its own a criminal contempt of court proceeding. A jail sentence may be the result.

PROHIBITIONS AGAINST LAW SUITS

Like criminal "double jeopardy," a similar prohibition exists in the common law for suits of a civil nature. Mr. S cannot sue Mr. B for the contract price once the appeal in the highest court has been decided in Mr. B's favor, or the time-limit for appeal has expired. Should Mr. S attempt to sue him, Mr. B need only show that there has already been a "former adjudication on the merits" (on the real issues) and the judge will dismiss the complaint. The suit is said to be barred by the doctrine of "*res judicata*" (Latin for "things already decided"). Were there not such a rule, no one would ever know when a law suit was finally ended. *Res judicata* says that the end must occur after the final judgment.

Another very important prohibition against law suits is the "statute of limitations." These laws provide a certain time period within which a law suit may be brought. If the plaintiff does not bring the action within that time period he is forever barred from pressing his claim. For example, the state statute of limitations on the contract action which Mr. S brought to court was two years. Fortunately, he filed his complaint a few weeks after Mr. B refused to pay him. Had he waited more than two years, however, he could not have sued at all.

Statutes of limitations have different time periods for different purposes. Many criminal limitations statutes provide that the state must institute a proceeding within seven years of the commission of the crime. Statutes of limitations serve the purpose of forcing a suit when the evidence and the claim are relatively fresh and the chances of a judgment based on mistake or fraud are less.

Part IV: The Jury

The jury system is one of the most significant parts of American law. Throughout the centuries people have argued and fought wars over the right to a jury trial. Why all the fuss?

The 12-member jury is usually traced back to England's King John and the Magna Carta in 1215. The English used a number system based on 12, rather than the decimal system, and this fact probably accounts for the present number of jury members. But this and the fact that verdicts must be unanimous are perhaps the only features we have inherited from those early days.

Originally, jury members were chosen from the area in which the crime was committed if they knew something about the incident. They were simply *witnesses*, sworn to tell the truth of the facts in the case. The trial jury today is just the opposite of the old "witness jury": jurors are not supposed to know anything about the people involved or the incident but are supposed to be an impartial panel, deciding upon the facts of the case by following the formal procedures of the courtroom.

Juries today are usually chosen from lists of eligible voters of the community. Although they might find it interesting to serve on a jury, many people try to avoid jury duty. Some are exempted because they have jobs which the legislature thinks are incompatible with serving on a jury (such as lawyers) or jobs that are more important. Jury duty takes time away from regular work, and the salary paid for a day in the jury box is rather small. Nevertheless, a large segment of judicial proceedings depends upon the jury. And, obviously, a jury is only as good as the people who compose it.

Before being selected, potential jurors must be questioned by plaintiff's and defendant's lawyers, in the presence of a court official, as we have seen. Since the jury ultimately will decide who will win the case, neither party wants a juror who is prejudiced against him. In *theory* the final jury will be impartial. For a number of reasons, it doesn't always work out that way in practice. Potential jurors may not answer the lawyers' questions truthfully, or may not realize they have a personal interest in the case until later. Or, the jurors may honestly believe they are not prejudiced, but in fact find that they are after the trial is in progress. To reduce the chances of this occurring, most states allow each lawyer, in addition to challenges for cause, a certain number of "peremptory challenges" at the *voir dire* in criminal cases. (Each lawyer can arbitrarily reject a given number of potential jurors for any reason whatsoever.) But when the lawyers exhaust their challenges the task of shaping the jury is left to the court.

JUDGE'S CONTROL OF THE JURY

Just as the court has an important say in who shall be on the jury, so the judge has an important role to play in deciding what the jury can say. We have already seen how the judge instructs the jury to apply the law to the facts which the jury finds. He also has a number of other control devices at his disposal during the trial.

Directing and Reversing the Jury

If the evidence is not sufficient to permit a jury to find for the plaintiff on any reasonable grounds, the judge may "direct a verdict" for the defendant in a civil trial. In a negligence case, for instance, if a plaintiff's entire case rested on his own statement that the defendant had struck him, without any evidence of negligence, the plaintiff will not have "sustained his burden of proof" and a verdict will be directed for the defendant.

If the jury returns with a verdict in a civil case which the judge thinks is so wrong that the jury must have been thinking unreasonably, he can grant a judgment for the other party. This is called a "judgment n.o.v." (from the Latin, *non obstante verdicto*, "notwithstanding the verdict"). Rather than grant a directed verdict the judge may prefer to let the jury decide the case on the reasonable chance that it will decide the issue in the proper way. If it does not, the judge may then grant a judgment n.o.v.

Suppose the trial judge is wrong? The appellate court will simply reverse his judgment and reinstate the jury verdict. Had the judge granted the directed verdict instead, a whole new trial would have been necessary, since a directed verdict stops the trial before the case ever goes to the jury.

A New Trial

Sometimes the judge will decide that a verdict is "against the weight of the evidence." There has been evidence supporting the winning party, but it was weak compared to the losing party's evidence. The judge will therefore grant the losing party's motion for a new trial as a matter of fairness.

Directed verdicts and judgments n.o.v. (in civil trials), and the order of a new trial (in both civil and criminal trials) are the three chief ways in which a judge can control the jury. But he must be careful not to use these devices indiscriminately. In fact, he must always "second-guess" the higher level court, because if his reason for using one of the controls is legally insufficient, he will be reversed if an appeal is taken.

SPECIAL VERDICTS

The questions of fact which juries must decide are usually complex. They often involve inferences about a person's state of mind from a mass of conflicting testimony. Was the driver careless? Did the defendant have the state of mind at the time of the shooting that is necessary according to the law for a murder conviction? In Mountebank's trial the jurors were required to decide whether Mountebank did steal, and if he did, whether he did so "feloniously." The jury in *State v. Mountebank* had to wrestle with the meaning of that term and others.

Although debate in the jury room is supposed to be entirely secret, enough jurors have explained what has happened during their deliberations to give researchers a fairly accurate picture of what goes on behind the closed doors. Here are what might have been some of the juror's comments in the Mountebank case:

"I certainly hope we decide this soon. I have to get home to cook supper for my husband and his boss," said one lady, who during the trial had been preparing the menu in her mind.

"We'll get it done when we're all agreed one way or the other," the foreman replied. "A man's liberty is at stake."

"I say he did it," said a gentleman at one end of the table. "He didn't have an alibi."

"Yes he did; he said he was walking in the park," another juror rejoindered.

"But who was with him? No one. You can't believe a robber."

"We don't know that he's a robber—that's what we're supposed to decide."

"I say if he did it before, he'd do it again."

"The judge said that his past record doesn't prove anything about *this* case."

"Well, I read in the newspaper that he's guilty," said another.

"That's for us to decide, not the paper."

"Well, I don't know, the paper seemed to make sense," was the answer.

Unfortunately, some juries are like this, and do not fully understand what the judge has said or do not listen to his instructions carefully. To prevent such befuddled thinking from entering into a decision, the judge may in some states ask the jury in a civil trial for a series of "special verdicts." Rather than require the jurors to decide on a "general verdict" for plaintiff or defendant, the judge will ask the jury a number of separate questions:

"Do you think that it was the defendant's signature on the contract?"

"How much in earnings did the plaintiff lose because of his injuries?"

From the jury's answers to these special questions, the judge will award damages. In some very complex cases, it is easier for the judge to ask the separate questions than to try to explain to the jury the complicated set of laws which governs the case. However, special verdicts historically have never been used in criminal cases where the verdict is more serious.

WHEN JURIES ARE USED

The consensus of generations of practical politicians, political philosophers, legal scholars, and lawyers has been that it is better for 12 men and women to debate guilt or innocence openly among themselves rather than entrust the responsibility to a judge. The judge does not have to justify his conclusion to anyone but himself. He is but one man, and he may judge people and situations by his own personal rules of probability, based on his own experiences during years of consulting with attorneys. It is said that he may grow out of touch with community standards (e.g., what is reasonable behavior?) after long years on the bench. Some people, on the other hand, believe that a panel of judges should sit as a trial court to determine fact.

The jury system is not the only system. In continental European countries and in Latin America, juries are, for the most part, not used at all. Even in England and the United States there are numerous occasions when juries are not used either. The Constitution requires juries for all federal criminal trials as do the state constitutions for the trial of all felonies and most misdemeanors. But the defendant can always "waive" his right to a jury trial and agree to have a judge try the case, except in "capital cases" (where the sentence may be death). If a jury is waived, the judge will decide both the questions of law and the questions of fact.

Juries are not used nearly so often in civil trials as in criminal trials. One reason is that plaintiffs and defendants are more willing to waive their rights to a jury trial to save time. Another reason is that the federal and state constitutions guarantee jury trials in one class of civil case only: that of *common law*.

Centuries ago in England, two separate systems of law developed. Common law courts—those which would grant money judgments—used juries. A separate juryless court system was called "equity" because it was developed to remedy the harsh outcome of some cases in which common law judgments were not fair or equitable. Remedies such as specific performance, injunction, and reformation were granted by courts of equity (and hence are called "equitable remedies").

Even though today all federal courts and almost all state courts exercise both common law and equity powers (and thus can grant money judgments or injunctions), for historical reasons, juries are used only in cases which long ago would have been brought to a common law court. So today, if a plaintiff wants an injunction to stop his neighbor from using dynamite, a judge alone will hear the case, not a jury.

Because juries are not everywhere constitutionally required, some juries consist of less than 12 persons and may decide facts by a less than unanimous vote, in order to save time. But their use is rare; constitutional juries must have 12 members deciding the facts unanimously. (Whenever juries are unable to arrive at a unanimous agreement, the judge must dismiss the jury and order a new trial. A deadlocked jury, unable to agree on a verdict, is known as a "hung jury.")

Where jury trials are a matter of constitutional right, the rights of individual citizens will be secured not only by responsible government officials, but also by fellow citizens acting as responsible and attentive jurors to see in each case that justice is done.

Part V: The Court System

Because of a fundamental disagreement while the Constitution was being written in the late 1780's, there are two entirely different sets of laws in the United States today. The disagreement was between those who favored one central government and those who wanted the colonies (as states) to remain supreme. In the end, a compromise was worked out. The states gave up some of their powers, but limited the actions of the federal government by keeping a great deal of power for themselves.

The states and the federal government can each pass different sets of laws. The Constitution says, for instance, that only Congress can make laws regulating coinage or national commerce among the states; only Congress can make laws dealing with the armed services.

Over some other matters Congress has no regulatory authority at all. For instance, most laws dealing with traffic problems, and many laws dealing with business are state-determined. Problems arise however when the federal and state governments come into conflict.

The court system—the judiciary—is the organ of government which decides when the states have passed laws beyond their power or when Congress has gone beyond its power. Earlier we saw how courts settle disputes between individuals. Now we will see how the court system works to settle disputes between the states and the federal government.

A court is like an octopus. It has many arms which reach out and touch many things. The courts within the court system are connected to each other by means of these arms.

To go along with the two separate sets of laws (state and federal), there are two different court systems in every community in the United States. They are arranged like a pyramid of octopuses. At the top is the United States Supreme Court; in the middle are the state and federal appellate courts, and at the bottom are the state and federal trial courts.

State judges in most cases do not have to be concerned with federal law, federal judges in most cases do not have to be concerned about state law.

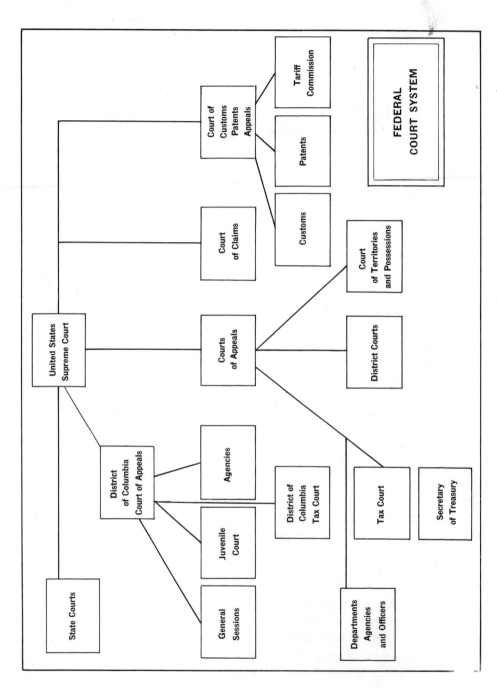

FEDERAL COURT SYSTEM

United States Supreme Court

State Courts

District of Columbia Court of Appeals

Courts of Appeals

Court of Claims

Court of Customs Patents Appeals

General Sessions

Juvenile Court

Agencies

District of Columbia Tax Court

District Courts

Court of Territories and Possessions

Customs

Patents

Tariff Commission

Tax Court

Secretary of Treasury

Departments Agencies and Officers

Yet sometimes state courts must use federal law; sometimes federal courts must use state law. In some cases, a person may legally choose to bring his case either to the state court or to the federal court. How these two court systems operate side by side without continual conflict is a significant chapter in the story of American federalism.

THE FEDERAL COURT SYSTEM

The only federal court which is mentioned specifically in the Constitution is the Supreme Court. All the others—and there are more than 100—were created by Congress and could be abolished tomorrow if Congress so desired.

It is highly unlikely, though, that Congress will ever abolish them. The number of cases—the "caseload"—which confronts the federal courts each year totals more than 100,000, and judicial calendars in many states are so crowded that it takes years before a case can come to trial.

District Courts

At the first level of the federal judicial system is the trial court. There are 86 federal districts in the United States, and in each sits one "district court." The tentacles of this judicial octopus reach out to the district boundary line, and in some cases a little beyond. It is here that the vast amount of federal litigation begins and here that most of it is disposed of.

All federal courts are governed by one set of rules written by special judicial committees, approved by the U.S. Supreme Court, and passed into law by Congress. Thus, whether you are in Alaska, Florida, Hawaii, Kansas, New York, or Puerto Rico, the procedures are the same. The summons must be served in the same way, the defendant must answer the complaint within 20 days, and so on. Very often, however, federal procedures differ from those used in state courts.

The judicial tentacles of the district courts are kept busy. One arm can mete out fines and jail sentences in criminal cases. Another arm can order money judgments in civil suits. Still another arm can issue injunctions in certain cases. The district court can order the taxpayer to pay his taxes, and it can order the Treasury Department of the United States to refund taxes when the Department has collected too much. It can appoint a person called a "receiver" to take over a bankrupt business in order to manage the company's final affairs. One of the trial court's arms extends into jails, and another arm can admit foreigners to United States citizenship.

Behind these judicial tentacles sit the "district judges." Each court has from 1 to 24 judges, depending on the population in the district and the volume of work. The Chief Justice of the United States has the authority to transfer judges from one district to another temporarily, to help where there is an overload of work. More than 350 judges serve at the district level. They, like all federal judges at all levels, are appointed for life terms by the President subject to approval by a majority vote of the Senate.

Courts of Appeal or Circuit Courts

Standing above the district courts are the Courts of Appeal. They are arranged in 11 "circuits." Each circuit has from three to nine judges, who consider all appeals from the district courts lying within the circuit. Whenever a person loses a case in a district court, he has the right to appeal to his circuit court of appeals.

The judicial tentacles of the circuit courts cover a very wide area. They can review cases on appeal from the district courts, and if proper, they can issue orders to the district courts, to the United States Government and its officials, to private individuals and companies, to states, and to special courts. The circuit courts, like the district courts, have the power to rule laws unconstitutional, subject to review by the United States Supreme Court.

Special Courts and Agencies

In addition to these three court levels, there are some special courts within the federal system: among these are the Tax Court, the Court of Customs and Patent Appeals, and the Court of Claims (for suits claiming money from the federal government).

There are also a great number of administrative agencies which have been given judicial tentacles by Congress. There are many kinds of activities which Congress or a state legislature does not have the time to carry on: for instance, making sure that food is properly packaged and inspected for cleanliness cannot be supervised closely by Congress. So Congress has created the Federal Trade Commission and the Food and Drug Administration to make sure that the consumer is protected. These agencies, by acting on a case-by-case basis, develop experience in consumer affairs.

Many of these agencies act as courts. The National Labor Relations Board, for instance, has been given jurisdiction by Congress to issue rulings in disputes between labor unions and business employers. It tries to see that the worker receives every right the law gives him. The losing party may request review by the proper court of appeal.

We will look at the third and highest level of the national judicial system, the Supreme Court, after we have examined the state court system a little more closely.

THE STATE COURTS

State court systems are not organized on as logical a basis as the federal judiciary. This is partly because politics and traditions within a state are different from those of Congress, and partly because the court reform movement which has affected federal courts has not yet reached deep into local communities.

Although the form of organization is different in the various states, most states have four separate levels to their judicial pyramid. These levels are the "municipal" court or the "justice of the peace" court; the "intermediate" court; the "superior" or "county" court; and the state "supreme" court.

Municipal Courts

The court of the justice of the peace is most commonly found in rural areas. In sizable communities, municipal courts (often called "police courts" or "magistrates courts") perform the same kind of work. The justice of the peace handles petty civil suits (where the value involved is not more than $100 or so) and very minor crimes, such as breaches of the peace. Among their other duties, justices of the peace are usually authorized to perform marriages. Justices of the peace and judges of municipal courts are usually elected officials.

Large cities, such as New York, Chicago and Philadelphia, have established divisions of their municipal courts to deal with special areas—traffic, small claims (involving sums under a certain set limit, usually $200 to $300), juvenile offenders, and marriage and divorce. The judicial tentacles of these special courts extend only to their own area. They are said to be courts of "special jurisdiction" in contrast to federal district courts and state superior courts which, because they can handle many kinds of cases, are called courts of "general jurisdiction." By working in a court with a special area, municipal judges develop skills in these fields and are better able to administer justice efficiently.

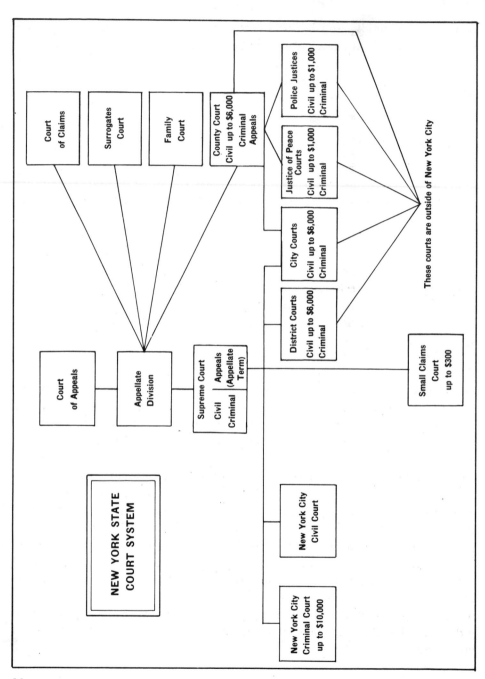

NEW YORK STATE COURT SYSTEM

Court of Appeals

Appellate Division

Supreme Court — Civil / Criminal | Appeals (Appellate Term)

Court of Claims

Surrogates Court

Family Court

County Court — Civil up to $6,000 / Criminal / Appeals

Police Justices — Civil up to $1,000 / Criminal

Justice of Peace Courts — Civil up to $1,000 / Criminal

City Courts — Civil up to $6,000 / Criminal

District Courts — Civil up to $6,000 / Criminal

Small Claims Court up to $300

New York City Civil Court

New York City Criminal Court up to $10,000

These courts are outside of New York City

Intermediate Courts

Many states have courts at a level higher than municipal courts but lower than the general trial courts. These intermediate courts are generally organized on a county basis, but perform much the same kind of work as the municipal courts. Often the plaintiff has a choice of going to a municipal or intermediate court. In any event, he can usually appeal to a third level court (not an appellate court but a court of original jurisdiction which can try cases begun in lower courts), which will begin a new trial and ignore what the lower court did. This is known as an appeal "*de novo*" (Latin for "starting afresh").

General Trial Court

The third level is the general trial court. This is the court in which most cases begin. These courts are usually called "county" or "superior" courts. They may be arranged by county or by judicial districts which include more than one county, whichever the state legislature has determined. With some exceptions, these are the only state courts which use a jury. Judges of these courts are elected in 34 states, most often for four-year terms. But these and higher judges almost always have had formal training in law schools, in contrast to many magistrates and justices of the peace, who have not.

About one-fourth of the states have a level between the superior (trial) court and the highest state court. These are the appellate courts, and they are like the federal courts of appeals, except that the judges are almost always elected. Three or more judges sit in the appellate court of each district established by the state legislature. Juries are not used here; only questions of law are settled.

State Supreme Courts

The fourth level (or fifth level in roughly 15 states which have appellate courts) is the state supreme court. (Curiously enough, New York State calls its general trial courts "supreme" courts, but they are not supreme. Its highest court is the Court of Appeals.)

But by whatever name they are called, there are courts of last resort within each state. Once the five or seven judges who sit on the benches of these high courts have decided a case the only recourse left to a disappointed party is the United States Supreme Court (and then, only in certain, special cases). The state supreme courts are responsible for settling all questions of state law; they speak the final word on the state constitution. No one, not even the United States Supreme Court, can change their interpretation of their own state's constitution (although the Supreme Court can declare a section of the state constitution invalid if it conflicts with the Federal Constitution). The state supreme courts have the power to reverse all other state courts in their state.

JUDICIAL POWER OF THE COURTS

There are over 1,000 courts in the United States. Which courts decide which cases? This is an important question because the power to decide what a statute means or whether a statute is constitutional is the power of control—power over governors and the President, legislatures, and other courts.

Which judicial tentacles are stronger, then? Are federal courts more powerful than state courts, or can state courts override federal courts? The answer is, as we might expect, that in some areas the state courts are more powerful than federal courts, and in other areas, the reverse is true.

Judicial power is the power of a court to decide a case by judicial methods. But a court must have "jurisdiction" over a case (the authority to hear it) before it can hear it and exercise its judicial power.

Article III, Section 2 of the Constitution spells out the five broad areas in which the federal courts *may* (if Congress authorizes them to) exercise their judicial power:

1. Cases involving "federal questions"—that is, cases which arise when someone claims protection or benefit of the Constitution, federal laws, or treaties. Among these laws are federal criminal laws, interstate commerce laws, and copyright laws.

2. Cases involving admiralty and maritime matters. These are matters relating to oceans and navigable lakes and rivers, such as crimes committed aboard ships, torts committed at sea, and commercial shipping laws (such as contracts concerning ships).

3. Cases involving the federal government. If you sue the federal government for money it owes you, or the government sues you for income taxes you owe, the federal courts have the power to decide the case.

4. Cases between citizens of different states. One-quarter of all civil suits tried in federal courts (nearly 15,000 cases a year) are there because of this "diversity jurisdiction" (so called because there must be a diversity of citizenship between the parties).

5. Cases involving citizens of the same state who claim that different states gave them deeds to the same piece of land.

(There are a few other kinds of cases which can be decided by the Supreme Court, but not by the lower federal courts.)

In each of these five areas, the federal courts have judicial power. This means that if such cases are brought to the federal courts, they have the power to make a decision and order a judgment for one side or the other. This is as far as the power extends, however. It is up to the President to see that the decisions of the federal courts are enforced, just as it is up to the governors of each state to see that the decisions of the state court are enforced. If the parties involved fail to follow the court's orders and the President or governor refuses to enforce the decision, law and order break down, and freedom, which depends on justice, disappears. One of the principal reasons this country has remained the freest in the world is that our court decisions are usually obeyed, and if they are not obeyed immediately they are almost always enforced by the Chief Executive. If a decision is not liked, there are orderly ways in which to change the law for the future.

JURISDICTION OF THE COURTS

In order to hear a case in the first place, the court must have "jurisdiction," or the legal authority to hear it. The federal courts get their authority from Congress, so it is Congress that determines the cases that can come to trial in federal courts.

This is one of the many ways in which the checks and balances of the different branches of government come into operation. This is how Congress checks the courts' power to interpret the laws passed by Congress and to declare a law unconstitutional when necessary.

In 1869, for instance, when Congress thought the Supreme Court was going to reverse a lower court and didn't want it to do so, Congress simply passed a law that said the Supreme Court did not have jurisdiction over that particular case. Even though oral argument had already been heard, the Court instead of deciding the case, agreed that it had no jurisdiction and dismissed the suit. As a result, the lower court decision was upheld.

Congress rarely passes such a law, however. If it frequently did, our system of justice would be crippled because Congress could prevent our courts from giving equal justice to all by suspending jurisdiction whenever it pleased.

Certain kinds of cases, such as suits between two states, must *begin* in the

Supreme Court and not in a lower court. When a court has the power to review a case begun in a lower court it is said to have "appellate jurisdiction." When a suit may be started in a court it is said to have "original jurisdiction."

Originally, Congress allowed the federal courts to hear only a few kinds of cases. Over the years, however, Congress has come to understand the wisdom of allowing the courts to use their judicial power, and has given the federal courts almost all of the jurisdiction allowed by the Constitution. (Remember that the Constitution in Article III extends the judicial power to five classes of cases—Congress cannot give the courts more jurisdiction without an amendment to the Constitution.)

Federal

However, federal courts today still do not have as much jurisdiction as the Constitution would permit. For instance, the "federal question" jurisdiction is limited by the amount of money involved: if a case involves less than $10,000 it cannot be tried in federal court, but must go instead to the proper state court.

Some cases can be brought only to federal court. Congress by law has given exclusive jurisdiction to federal courts in cases concerning crimes against the United States; in cases which involve patent, copyright, and bankruptcy laws; and in cases in which the United States is a party.

State

Many cases, on the other hand, cannot be brought to federal court at all. Most criminal laws are enacted by state legislatures and are for state courts to handle. Traffic laws are under the jurisdiction of the states and local communities. Each state sets up its own standards of public health and safety. Doctors and lawyers, engineers and architects, for instance, must be licensed in each state before they can practice. Marriage and divorce laws are entirely state created and are not subject to Congressional interference. Laws relating to death, funerals, and wills are state matters. The disposition of property— who owns what and when—is regulated by the states. Suits for negligence and other torts are covered by state, not federal, law. Hundreds of other important topics—such as state election laws, county boundary lines, the length of term of state officials—are all under the sole discretion of the state legislatures, and the state courts generally have exclusive jurisdiction over cases involving these laws.

Concurrent Jurisdiction

But in a wide number of cases, federal and state courts share jurisdiction. State courts may hear cases involving many federal laws. Federal courts, as we have already seen, have "diversity jurisdiction"—the authority to hear and decide cases which involve citizens of different states. Thus, a New York citizen may sue a Texas citizen in a federal court in Texas, even if the case involves a state law.

In a momentous decision in 1938, the Supreme Court declared that from then on federal courts must use the *states'* interpretations of their own state laws. For almost a century prior to this 1938 decision, the federal courts had been using their own interpretations of state law.

A Mr. Tompkins was walking along the track of the Erie Railroad in Pennsylvania when a train came by and injured him. Because the railroad company had offices in New York State, he sued the company for negligence in federal court there. What was the basis for the jurisdiction of the federal court? Diversity of citizenship: Mr. Tompkins was a Pennsylvania citizen and under existing law the railroad company was considered a citizen of New York. The court did not follow the Pennsylvania rule, which said that the railroad was not responsible since Tompkins was contributorily negligent in walking along the track. Instead, the federal district court in New York decided that the common law of the United States required the railroad to pay Tompkins for his injuries, and the United States Court of Appeals for the Second Circuit affirmed the lower court.

The Supreme Court reversed the decision. It ruled in *Erie Railroad v. Tompkins* that there was no such thing in diversity cases as a general common law of the United States. The case which said there was, decided in the 1840's, was expressly overruled. The Supreme Court said that common law could only exist in each separate state. The federal court in New York should have used the state rule. So the case was sent back to the federal court in New York with the instructions to determine what the state rule was and to use it in the case.

That 1938 case was one of the most significant decisions ever made, concerning the nature of federalism, for it meant that federal courts must follow state law in diversity cases.

This decision works in reverse, too. Many questions of federal law may be taken to state court. A state court cannot devise federal law through its interpretations of federal statutes; it must respect the interpretations of the federal courts, because the "supremacy clause" of the Federal Constitution declares that federal law is supreme. Because of the double-pronged character of the *Erie* doctrine and the supremacy clause, what might otherwise be serious conflicts and crises are avoided.

Conflicts

Nevertheless, conflicts do arise within the federal judiciary. Different federal circuits may come to the opposite interpretations of the same federal statute, or to opposite conclusions as to whether a statute passed by Congress is constitutional.

Conflicts arise between the state and federal court systems. Federal courts may differ with various state courts on the meaning of federal or state law.

Conflicts may arise within the state judiciary. State laws may come into conflict with federal statutes or the Constitution, yet be upheld by state courts.

In all these cases, appeal is still possible to the Supreme Court of the United States. The nation's highest court stands ready to settle conflicts which may exist between the various courts or different laws.

JURISDICTION OVER THE PERSON

Before turning to the Supreme Court, there is one more kind of jurisdiction which we must look at, because ultimately the Supreme Court must settle the conflicts that arise here also.

The power of a court, just like the power of legislature, extends only to the boundaries of the state except in certain special cases. Thus, New York cannot make laws which tell Texans living in Texas what to do. Nor can a New York court make a ruling about a person who is living in Texas. Remember that a person must be served with personal notice that he is being sued; but an official of the court is only official so long as he is within the state boundary.

Although Congress could change the rule with respect to federal courts, the same rule is generally applicable. Thus, the jurisdiction of a federal court extends usually only to the state borders in which it sits. But because the federal courts are part of the United States Government, Congress *could* allow a district court in New York to take a case involving federal law between two California citizens, though for convenience's sake this is not in fact allowed.

The rules we have been looking at are valid as long as Texans stay in Texas or New Yorkers stay in New York. But suppose a Texan came to New York for a visit. If a New York sheriff could find him and serve him with a summons while he was in New York, he could be sued in New York. Even if the Texan went back to Texas before the trial, he would be under a legal obligation to be present at the New York trial.

If the Texan refused to come to the trial, the New Yorker, as the plaintiff, would go to court, point out to the judge that the defendant did not appear but that he was properly "served," and the judge would then give a "default" judgment for the plaintiff.

But the plaintiff still would not have his money, so he would then have to contact a lawyer in Texas (this can usually be done simply by calling or writing; a trip is unnecessary). The lawyer will then "sue on the judgment." Under the Constitution, each state must give "full faith and credit" to the court decisions of all other states. So the Texas court automatically would be bound to recognize the plaintiff as the winner, since he won his case in New York.

The lesson to be learned is obviously this: never ignore a summons, even if you are utterly certain you are in the right. Get a lawyer, or telephone your local legal aid bureau—an office in many communities which helps people in legal trouble. Then go to court and prove that you are right.

Many situations are extremely complicated. If you drive a car in a state in which you do not live and injure someone, you can be sued in that state even though you have not been handed a summons there (the Supreme Court settled this point). Since driving can be dangerous, and all states want to protect their citizens against injury, in return for the privilege of driving in neighbor states, you must risk the penalty of being sued there if you injure someone. The court must give you some notice that an "action" is being taken against you there, but it can mail you a notice; a court officer doesn't have to serve it personally.

If you own property in a state other than the one in which you live, the court can "attach" (hold, take and possibly sell) that property should someone sue you, subject to a proper trial. The court need not serve you personally with a summons to attach your property; if you do not come for the trial or you do not have a lawyer contest the attachment, your property will be sold.

But the dividing line between lawful and unlawful attachment or jurisdiction over the person is sometimes exceedingly thin. In these cases, as well as cases involving conflicts between laws and courts, disputes can be resolved finally only by the Supreme Court.

Part VI: The Supreme Court

On the last day of his term, March 3, 1801, President John Adams appointed many men of his party to federal judgeships. These men are sometimes called the "midnight judges," since Adams and his Secretary of State John Marshall (whom Adams had just appointed Chief Justice of the United States) continued to sign and deliver their commissions up to the stroke of 12 on the night Thomas Jefferson succeeded Adams as President. Adams was a Federalist who had been defeated by the Republican-Democratic candidate, Jefferson, and he was taking political revenge.

MARBURY v. MADISON

One of the midnight judges, Marbury, had been named justice of the peace of Washington County in the District of Columbia. Although his commission had been signed, there had not been time to deliver it, and President Jefferson's Secretary of State (later President), James Madison, refused to do so. Under the authority of a statute passed by Congress in 1789, Marbury sued in the Supreme Court for a "writ of mandamus" (a court order directing a public official to discharge an official duty).

Although the facts of the case seemed to lean directly in Marbury's favor, the Supreme Court was faced with a real dilemma. The Court was young and its authority had never been put to the test. If it ordered Madison to deliver the commission and President Jefferson ordered him not to, a grave conflict might result. If in its first major test the Court was shown to be powerless by being deliberately disobeyed, the President—the only man capable of enforcing the law—might well emerge as the dominant political force in America, with no possible "check and balance" by the Court. The Court's task under Marshall was to reach a fair and just result in the case and at the same time ensure that the decision of the Court would be obeyed and its power respected.

Marshall achieved these ends in a subtle and clever way. He first demonstrated that Marbury had a clear right to the commission. He then showed that the laws of the United States did afford Marbury a remedy. These two points were direct slaps at Jefferson. But he then said a *mandamus* issued by the Supreme Court was not the correct remedy, because the 1789 Act of Congress which gave Marbury the authority to sue was unconstitutional. While the Act permitted Marbury to *start* his suit in the Supreme Court, the Constitution, Marshall argued, did not give original jurisdiction to the Supreme Court in this kind of case. That is, under the Constitution the Supreme Court could only decide the case on appeal, after a decision had first been reached in a lower court. The Supreme Court had appellate, but not original, jurisdiction. And, reasoned Marshall, if the Constitution were to remain the supreme law of the land, a statute which conflicted with it could not be enforced.

Significance of the Case

What did Marshall accomplish? These things:

(1) The Court lost no power or respect, since its decision was certain to be obeyed. Because the Court simply dismissed the suit for lack of jurisdiction, Jefferson was not obliged to do anything.

(2) The Court had made the point that Marbury was legally entitled to the commission, but refused to order the Secretary of State to deliver it because the Court had no power to do that.

(3) The Court established its power to declare laws unconstitutional when they conflict with the Constitution. This was of the utmost importance. Since Jefferson had no alternative but to accept the decision, a valuable precedent was established.

(4) The Court established the rule that a decision as to whether a law is constitutional will only be made if there is no other ground on which to dispose of the case. This is an important rule since it limits the need for the Court to make sweeping pronouncements and preserves social stability.

Thus the Supreme Court quite early in its history settled its power to interpret the Constitution and to set aside laws in conflict with it. That 1803 case, *Marbury v. Madison*, 1 Cranch (5 U.S.) 137* was extremely important, for if the Supreme Court had not taken this opportunity to assume the power to declare unconstitutional laws invalid, the Constitution might simply have faded away. *Marbury v. Madison* also helped pave the way for other branches of government (Congress and the Executive) to accept the Court's equal and coordinate status. Checks and balances thus became a reality.

---

* Note the citation. Until 1876, the Supreme Court reports were cited by the name of the Court Reporter. Thus 1 Cranch 137 means that *Marbury v. Madison* is found at page 137 of the first volume published by William Cranch. The "5 U.S." in parentheses shows that it is in the fifth volume of the series of Supreme Court decisions. Beginning with the 91st volume, the reporter's name was dropped and the citation "U.S." used.

What happened to Marbury? Why didn't he bring another suit in a lower federal court, in which, according to Marshall, he would have found a proper remedy? Marbury's term of office was only five years, almost half of which had expired by the time his case was decided. Because the pay of the office was small, and because President Jefferson had already appointed new men to fill the positions of the "midnight judges," Marbury apparently felt it simply was not worth the trouble. So the matter ended.

JUDICIAL REVIEW

The process of interpretation of the Constitution is often called "judicial review." This name applies also to the interpretation of statutes, but it is at the constitutional level that the most attention has been focused, since a decision involving our Constitution strikes at the very roots of our nation and society. Of the thousands of laws passed every year by Congress and the state legislatures, very few have been declared unconstitutional. Since 1789, perhaps only 85 federal laws and some 750 state laws have been "voided" by the Supreme Court.

Nevertheless, from those early days to the present, the Supreme Court has been at the center of political controversy. Because the members of the court—the "Justices"—are chosen by the President, who naturally wants to see his political philosophy fostered on the bench, the Court's complexion changes as changes in popular sentiment result in the election of a President with different ideas and party affiliation. Since the Justices serve life terms, however, they almost always serve longer than the President, and often longer than the party which put them there. When President Lyndon B. Johnson took office, for example, he was faced with a court composed of two Justices named by President Franklin D. Roosevelt more than a quarter-century before, one named by President Harry Truman, four by President Dwight D. Eisenhower, and two by President John F. Kennedy. The fact that the membership of the Court is a product of political changes serves to promote debate and discussion within the Court and enables it to play an active role among American political institutions.

EVOLUTION OF THE COURT

With the changing membership has come a slow change in the Court's interests. During the 19th century, as America was expanding and developing, the Supreme Court concentrated its energies on questions of commerce, the national economy, and federalism. During the present century, the Court is turning increasingly to the protection of individual liberties.

Criticism is often heard that it is undemocratic to allow judges to make law, as happens when they reverse previous decisions or declare laws unconstitutional. Two of the Supreme Court's most controversial decisions in recent years went far toward "making law." In one case, *Brown v. Board of Education*, 347 U.S. 438 (1954), the Court held that public school segregation was unconstitutional under the 14th Amendment's command to the states that they must give equal protection of the laws to all their citizens. The Court held that separate school systems for whites and Negroes are not equal.

The Court recently used the "equal protection clause" in deciding another controversial issue: whether a state could have election districts which differ from each other in number of inhabitants. One state, for instance, was so divided that in one district a few thousand people elected a state senator and in another district hundreds of thousands of voters elected only one state senator. In *Reynolds v. Sims*, 377 U.S. 533 (1964), the Court declared that each district in a state must contain substantially the same number of people. Although many states were unhappy about this decision, most states under court order began to reapportion.

There is no doubt that many of the decisions of the Supreme Court are highly controversial. But it is *because* the issues are highly complex and controversial that they eventually reach the Supreme Court. Simple, noncontroversial cases, previously decided lower down on the judicial ladder, never reach the Court.

Is the Supreme Court always right? Undoubtedly not. But bear in mind Justice Robert Jackson's famous statement in 1953: "We are not final because we are infallible; but we are infallible only because we are final." Ultimately, difficult questions and bitter disputes must be answered or resolved and brought to an end. The Supreme Court is the final authority on judicial disputes. Non-judicial disputes still are settled by Congress, the President, the states, and the people.

CHECKS AND BALANCES

Democracy is not a static thing, but a process under which the system of checks and balances really does work. Should the court interpret a statute in a way in which Congress does not stand in agreement, Congress has the power to reverse the Court's decision by passing a new law. This in fact is almost

When the President addresses Congress, the third "coordinate but equal" branch of the federal government listens also. The Justices of the Supreme Court sit in the front row, dressed in their traditional judicial robes. For a system of checks and balances to work properly, no branch can be isolated from the other.

always what happens when a decision of the Supreme Court is not popular with Congress. In a democracy there are always open ends—ways in which changes can be made. For if enough people disagree with the Court's decision in a constitutional matter, the Constitution itself can be amended. This has happened on two occasions—both the 11th Amendment (referring to suits against a state) and the 16th Amendment (establishing the federal income tax) were passed in order to reverse decisions by the Court. Sometimes a later Supreme Court will reverse the Court's own earlier decisions.

RESTRAINTS

The Court has developed some of its own ground rules for the handling of constitutional issues. One rule we have already seen in connection with the Marbury case: the Court will never decide on constitutional grounds if there is presented some non-constitutional ground on which to base a decision. Other rules are:

1. The Court will dismiss a case when the parties to the suit are friendly (that is, when both sides want the same outcome). In other words, the Court will not approve or disapprove an action which is not disputed by one party.

2. The Court will dismiss a case if a litigant fails to show that he was injured by the law he is claiming is unconstitutional.
3. If the litigant has benefited from an allegedly unconstitutional law, the Court will not hear him.
4. Whenever an Act of Congress is questioned as unconstitutional, the Court will try to find a way to construe (interpret) it so that the question can be avoided.
5. If the Court cannot avoid formulating a rule of constitutional law, because there is no other just way to settle the case, the Court will make the rule as narrow as possible.

These purely self-imposed restraints keep the Court from handing down constitutional decisions very often. The Supreme Court thus allows other organs of government to work out solutions to problems where possible.

SUPREME COURT CASES

Only in a few cases of original jurisdiction has the Supreme Court handed down important decisions. By far the more talked-about decisions, of course, concern the Constitution and important federal laws. Remember that the vast majority of cases never reach the Supreme Court. In fact, the Supreme Court at its discretion can refuse to review all but a few types of cases:

(1) when a state law is declared unconstitutional by a *federal* court;

(2) when a *state* supreme court rules that a federal treaty or statute is unconstitutional; or

(3) when a *state* supreme court upholds a state law which the losing party contends is unconstitutional.

Except for these three kinds of cases, the Supreme Court may refuse all other appeals. Why? Thousands of cases are decided every year in the 11 federal circuits and the 50 state supreme courts, as well as in the Tax Court, the Court of Customs and Patent Appeals, and the administrative agencies. It is impossible for nine Justices to look fully into more than a small fraction of those cases.

Certiorari

Yet cases which are appealed as a matter of right do not constitute the bulk of the Court's work each term. (The "judicial term" begins in October and ends in early June.) Most of the cases (less than 300 each year) which the Court finally reviews on their merits come to it by way of a procedure known as "certiorari" (pronounced "sir-sher-air-eye" and often abbreviated and pronounced simply as "cert"). Whenever the Court "grants cert" it means simply that four out of the nine Justices think the case is important enough for the nation's highest court to decide. Certiorari is entirely discretionary: if the Court doesn't want to review a case, it doesn't have to.

Still, the Court is not permitted to review just any case at random. First, the losing party in a lower court must petition the Supreme Court for certiorari. Second, the case must involve a question of substantial importance; for example, the validity of a state or federal statute or a right claimed under federal law. If two circuit courts of appeal have made contrary rulings on the same federal law, the Supreme Court will grant certiorari in order to bring uniformity into the law. It obviously wouldn't be equitable to have federal law mean one thing in one state and a different thing in another. Or, if a state court has made an important ruling on a matter of federal law which has not previously come before the Supreme Court, the Court may well grant certiorari in order to review for itself a matter of great national importance.

Every time the Supreme Court accepts a petition of certiorari and agrees to review a case, it is acting in one of its principal roles: the organ of government which reduces conflicts between lower courts and brings uniformity into the interpretation of federal statutory or Constitutional law.

Even when the Court does not grant certiorari, it may well disagree with the ruling of the lower court, but the amount of time available to the Court is limited, so the Justices must select the most meaningful cases to review. Of the nearly 2,700 cases with which the Court deals each year, some two-thirds are refused certiorari. Even so, approximately 400 cases are left undecided for the next term, and some 200 are disposed of in other ways.

The workload of the Court is a heavy one, and the nine Justices do all the work themselves. Although each Justice has two law clerks (and the Chief Justice has three) to confer with and to help with research, the clerks make not a single decision. Furthermore, every case that comes to the Court for certiorari is reviewed by *all* nine Justices. Even the 1,700 cases which are denied certiorari must be reviewed before certiorari is denied. The remaining cases involve an enormous amount of time.

INSIDE THE SUPREME COURT BUILDING

Inside an immense marble structure, patterned on the Parthenon of ancient Athens, directly facing the Capitol in Washington, sits the nation's highest court. Fewer than 100 people are employed by the Court, including the nine Justices. In consequence, its huge corridors appear deserted compared to the Senate Office Buildings (which employ thousands) just down the street.

During arguments, the Justices sit in a central room on an elevated platform which holds the judicial bench. Just behind the bench are nine high-backed, but oddly-shaped chairs. Each chair is different, since it has been made to the individual Justice's specifications in a special workshop in the basement of the Court.

The central room is the only place where the Justices work in public. During arguments before the bench, seats for a few hundred people are available on a first-come, first-served basis. The darkness of the huge space, surrounded by large columns of marble, contrasts markedly with the outside of the building, which, at midday, makes one squint from the white glare of the sun beating down on it. But if the sun does not pierce the interior, the questions the justices ask are penetrating enough. For it is here that legal history is made. (Actually, the Court has been in its present building only since 1935; before that it met in a small room inside the Capitol building.)

Normally the Court works in two-week sittings. For two weeks the Justices hear oral arguments and for the next two weeks they consider among themselves the merits of the cases they have heard. For this purpose they sit in a small, ornate conference room around a long table with a green-felt top. Only the Justices are permitted to enter this room.

The opinion of the Court is written by the Chief Justice if he sides with the majority and wants to write it. If he is overburdened with the writing of opinions, he may ask another Justice to write the opinion.

Most decisions are individually signed by the Justice who wrote them, as are the concurring and dissenting opinions. (Sometimes, when all the Court is in agreement and the issues are not felt to require a full opinion, an unsigned "per curiam" decision is written—this means simply that the whole court concurs.) The Justices' opinions take into account the circumstances of the case, the language of the statute, American history, the nature of the age in which we live, the history of the statute, the intent of the legislators who passed the law, and the intent of the framers of the Constitution.

Opinions of the Court, before public announcement, are printed secretly

Yesterday in the U. S. Supreme Court

WASHINGTON, Feb. 21—In the Supreme Court of the United States today, the following proceeding were had.

CERTIORARI GRANTED

970—Federal Trade Commission, Petr., v. Dean Foods Company et al, pet for writ, of cert. to the United States Court of Appeals for the Seventh Circuit granted. Case placed on summary calendar and set for oral argument on Monday, March 28, 1966.

OPINIONS

38—Alfred D. Rosenblatt, petr., v. Frank P. Baer. On writ. of cert. to the Supreme Court of New Hampshire. Judgment reversed and case remanded to the Supreme Court of New Hampshire for further procedings not inconsistent with the opinion of the court. Opinion by Justice Brennan. Concurring opinion by Justice Douglas. Concurring opinion by Justice Stewart. Opinion by Justice Black with whom Justice Douglas joined, concurring in part and dissenting in part. Opinion by Justice Harlan concurring in part and dissenting in part. Dissenting opinion by Justice Fortas. Justice Clark concurred in the result.

11—William T. Graham et al., petrs., v. John Deere Co. of Kansas City et al.;

37—Calmar, Inc., ptr., v. Cook Chemical Company; and

43—Colgate-Palmolive Company, petr., v. Cook Chemical Company. On wrils. of cert. to the United States Court of Appeals for the Eighth Circuit. Judgment in No. 11 affirmed. Judgment in Nos. 37 and 43 reversed and cases remanded to the United States District Court for the Western District of Missouri for further proceedings in conformity with the opinion of this court. Opinion by Justice Clark. Justice Stewart took no part in the consideration or decision in Nos. 37 and 43. Justice Fortas did not participate.

55—United States, Petnr., v. Bert N. Adams et al. On writ. of cert. to the United States Court of Claims. Judgment affirmed. Opinion by Justice Clark. Justice White dissents. Justice Fortas did not participate.

45—William C. Linn, pttr., v. United Plant Guard Workers of America, Local 114, et al. On writ. of cert. to the United States Court of Appeals for the Sixth Circuit. Judgment reversed and case remanded to the United States District Court for the Western District of Michigan for further proceedings in conformity with the opinion of this court. Opinion by Mr. Justice Clark. Dissenting opinion by Justice Black, Dissenting opinion by Justice Fortas with whom the Chief Justice and Justice Douglas joined.

792—Louisville & Nashville Railroad Co. v. United States et al. Appeal from the United States District Court for the Western District of Kentucky. Per curiam. Motions to affirm granted and judgment affirmed.

812—Hemphill et Us., Esc. v. Washington State Tax Commission. Appeal from the Supreme Court of Washington. Per curiam. Motion to dismiss granted and appeal dismissed for want of a substantial Federal question.

836—Nolan v. Rhodes, Governor of Ohio, et al. Appeal from the United States District Court for the Southern District of Ohio. Per curiam. Motion to affirm granted and judgment affirmed. Justice Fortas did not participate.

ORDERS IN PENDING CASES

132—Holt v. Kirby. Motion of Randolph Phillips for leave to file a brief, as amicus curiae, granted. Motion of Randolph Phillips for leave to participate in oral argument, as amicus curiae, denied. Justice Fortas did not participate.

318—Burns v. Richardson.

323—Cravalho v. Richardson

409—Abe v. Richardson. Motion of Harold S Roberts for leave to file a brief, as amicus curiae, granted. Motion of Harold S Roberts for leave to participate in the oral argument, as amicus curiae, denied. Justice Fortas did not participate.

490—Sheppard v. Maxwell. Motion of John T. Corrigan for leave to participate in the oral argument, as amicus curiae, denied.

545—Joseph E. Seagram & Sons, Inc. v. Hostetler. Motion of Wine and Spirits Wholesalers of America, Inc., for leave to file a brief, as amicus curiae, granted.

584—California v. Stewart

759—Miranda v. Arizona

760—Vignera v. New York

761—Westover v. United States

762—Johnson v. New Jersey

Motion of the respondent to dismiss the writ of cert. in No. 584 denied. Motion of the National District Attorneys Assn. for leave to participate in the oral argument, as amicus curiae, granted and 15 minutes are allotted for that purpose. Motion of the Attorney General of New York for leave to participate in the oral argument, as amicus curiae, is granted and 15 minutes are allotted for that purpose. Joint motion of counsel in No. 762 to remove this case from the Summary Calendar is granted and 15 additional minutes are allotted to each side.

597—Mills v. Alabama. Motion of the Alabama Press Assn. et al. for leave to participate in the oral argument, as amici curiae, denied.

847—Katzenbach v. Morgan

877—New York City Board of Elections v. Morgan. Motion of the appellees for leave to proceed in forma pauperis granted.

APPEALS—JURISDICTION NOTED

789—United States v. National Steel Corp.

860—United States v. Fabrizio

CERTIORARI GRANTED

346—Canada Packers, Ltd. v. Atchison, Topeka & Santa Fe Rwy Co.

869—Reider v. Michigan Sugar Co.

876—N.L.R.B. v. Acme Industrial Co.

950—Bank of Marin v. England

652—Transportation - Communication Employees Union v. Union Pacific RR. Co. Motion for leave to file supplemental pet. for writ of cert. granted.

CERTIORARI DENIED

397—United States v. American Broadcasting-Paramount Theatres, Inc.

698—Campbell v. United States

781—Tennessee Burley Tobacco Growers' Assn. v. Commodity Credit Corp.

791—Arrington v. Ohio

793—Fowler v. United States

821—Indiviglio v. United States

830—Grand River Dam Authority v. National Gypsum Co.

837—Bowling v. United States

839—Mutual Benefit Health & Accident Assn. v. Messina

840—Straub v. United States

842—Rosen v. United States

843—Ginsburg v. Ginsburg

845—Tippett v. United States

857—Burgdorf v. California

858—Hanover Ins. Co. v. Chrysler Corp.

862—Knoll v. Knoll

863—Jones v. Faconi

866—Necchi Sewing Machine Sales Corp. v. Necchi S.P.A.

867—Cohen v. Joseph

871—Butler v. United States

873—Wabash Fire & Casualty Ins. Co. v. United States.

878—Douglas v. Wirtz

879—Glazer v. Bove

881—Boys Town, U.S.A., Inc. v. World Church

882—Hawley v. Virginia

883—United States v. Black Diamond SS Corp.

885—Smith v. Illinois

886—Barnes v. Rederi A/B Fredrika

895—Robinson v. Humble Oil & Refining Co.

897—Fizitz, Inc. v. Patterson

899—Southwest Potash Corp. v. United States

912—Cozzi v. United States

919—Fowless v. State Tax Commission of New York

953—Franzblau v. Soles

962—Emory v. California

681—Robinson v. United States. Motion for

leave to file supplemental pet. for writ of cert. granted.

777—Coral Gables First National Bank v. American Surety Co. of New York. Motion of the respondent, American Surety Co. of New York, for assessment of damages denied.

838—Duesing v. Udall. Justice Fortas did not participate.

852—Chicago, Burlington & Quincy RR. Co. v. Illinois Commerce Commission. Justice Fortas did not participate.

859—2000 Plastic Tubular Cases, etc. v. United States. Motion to dispense with printing the pet. for writ of cert. granted.

933—Mancusi v. Hetenyi. Motion of respondent for leave to proceed in forma pauperis granted.

LEAVE TO FILE PETITIONS FOR WRITS OF HABEAS CORPUS DENIED

407 Misc.—Williams v. California Adult Authority.

1075 Misc.—Wood v. Boles.

1079 Misc.—Hochberg v. California

1097 Misc.—In the matter of application of Daup.

1105 Misc.—White v. Director.

1108 Misc.—Lynch v. United States.

1130 Misc.—Long v. Boles.

1170 Misc.—Cervantes v. United States.

1174 Misc.—Greathouse v. Boles.

LEAVE TO FILE PETITIONS FOR WRITS OF MANDAMUS DENIED

1064 Misc.—Minchella v. Levin.

1106 Misc.—Schack v. Roberts.

1052 Misc.—Schack v. Simpson. Motion for leave to file a pet. for writ of mandamus and/or prohibition and for other relief denied.

LEAVE TO FILE PETITION FOR WRIT OF PROHIBITION DENIED

1109 Misc.—Mortion v. Kansas.

REHEARINGS DENIED

432—Holmes v. Edcy.

614—Nehring v. Gerrity.

616—Easter v. Ziff.

632—Scalza v. United States.

660—Jones v. United States.

709—Muth v. Atlass.

733—Darr v. Atlass. Motion of the American Trial Lawyers Assn. for leave to file a brief, as amicus curiae, in support of the pet. for rehearing granted.

1 Misc.—Stello v. Pennsylvania.

15 Misc.—Gillentine v. United States.

668 Misc.—Trantino v. New Jersey.

697 Misc.—Bowden v. California Adult Authority.

772 Misc.—Vioa v. Roth.

773 Misc.—Skolnick v. Hallett.

794 Misc.—Eskridge v. Rhay.

807 Misc.—Furtak v. New York.

838 Misc.—McGann v. Richardson.

898 Misc.—McIntosh v. United States.

978 Misc.—Zanca v. Maimonides Hospital.

1044 Oct. Term 1962—Wapnick v. United States. Motion for leave to file second petitions for rehearing denied. Justice Fortas did not participate.

494 Oct. Term 1964—Brotherhood of R. Trainmen v. Louisville & Nashville R. Co. Motion for leave to file second petitions for rehearing denied. Justice Fortas did not participate.

402 Misc.—Fjellhammer v. United States.

518 Misc.—Birdsell v. United States.

524 Misc.—Hernandez v. California.

ORAL ARGUMENT

318—John A. Burns, Governor of the State of Hawaii, appellant, v. William S. Richardson Et Al.;

323—Elmer F. Cravalho Et Al., appellants, v. William S. Richardson Et Al.; and

409—Kazuhisa Abe Et Al., appellants, v. William S Richardson Et Al. Three hours allowed for oral argument.

Adjourned until Wednesday, Feb. 23, 1966, at 10 o'clock.

The day call for Wednesday, Feb. 23, 1966, will be as follows: Nos. 545, 341, 396 and 656.

Report from The New York Times.

in the Court's own basement printery. No one sees them but the printers, the Justices, their clerks, and secretaries. The opinions are circulated for comment and changes, and those who disagree may write dissenting opinions. Sometimes an opinion will be drafted 30 times before its author is satisfied.

Decisions used to be announced only on Mondays—known as "Decision Mondays," but because so many decisions have been handed down in recent years and because it is important that newspaper reporters have a chance to study the decisions in detail, decisions are now announced on other days during the week.

Although the Supreme Court term ends in June, work does not cease. Petitions for certiorari and appeal come pouring in, regardless of the temperature outdoors, and the Justices must examine some 60 or more every week. The Justices receive a six-week vacation before each new term begins, but often judicial work must be done even then.

In spite of occasional shortcomings over the years and the increasingly heavy workload, the process by which we entrust our Constitution to interpretation by the courts has worked fairly well. It must not be forgotten that our Constitution is now almost 200 years old. It was written by men who lived in a world without electricity, automobiles, television, telephones, indoor plumbing, or atomic bombs. It was a world which knew nothing of mass-produced jellies or of traffic jams. It was a world in which science was a rarity, medicine was crude, and the population was very small.

The fact that we are still living under the same Constitution attests to the brilliance of the Founding Fathers, but it also attests to the genius of the American judicial system. We live under the same Constitution not because its framers foresaw everything in detail, but rather because the document was left loose and flexible enough that Supreme Court justices through the years could interpret it in the light of the changes that took place in the United States, and breathe into it the life that enables it to remain our fundamental law.

Part VII: Court Problems

Many hundreds of years ago, the law was a crude, almost barbaric affair. Kings and lords did just what they wanted; might made right. But as society became more complicated and individual communities in England began to form a nation, the idea of a rational law began to develop. Royal proclamations were published, and Parliament passed statutes. If the spirit of the law was not followed, at least the form of the law was. Kings and judges began to feel that they must justify what they were doing. Logic and reason began to govern, not the ruthless power of a king. The idea of law was taking hold. Today in America (as in England and other countries too) people are ruled for the most part by law. We do more than pay lip service to the idea of law—it is fundamental to our society.

Nevertheless, our judicial system is not perfectly developed. There are still serious problems in the administration of justice about which men of good faith have engaged in lengthy and heated debate. There are no ready answers. The problems are presented here in the hope that the reader will profitably give a few hours to reading about them, thinking about them, discussing them, and debating them.

SOME GENERAL PROBLEMS
Cost

One major problem is the cost of obtaining justice in the courts. Many a justifiable complaint is dropped because the client does not have the money to pay for an attorney, for litigation and, especially, for appeal. Large organizations have the money, so that the scales of justice are often unbalanced in favor of the party with money.

In criminal cases, the state is obliged to provide a lawyer to defend an accused who is without funds. In civil cases, legal aid societies in some states have been extremely helpful in directing people without funds to take the proper legal action and in providing them with attorneys for counsel and litigation.

It is, nevertheless, true that rich people are able to hire better lawyers than poor ones. Money may not be able to buy justice, but it can win a lawsuit. Of course, every facet of life is to some extent limited by lack of money. Some people argue that we cannot make ease in getting to court equal for all, any more than we assure everyone the same income. Others argue that we shouldn't draw such a conclusion until we've tried harder to realize the great goal, whose words are chiseled in the marble of the Supreme Court, of guaranteeing "equal justice under law."

Lack of Sufficient Courts

A second problem is that we lack sufficient courts. Court calendars are so clogged in some federal districts and states that it takes years to get a case to trial. Some have argued that more courts would simply mean even more delays, since people who now settle their disputes out of court would be encouraged to litigate in court. While this may be true, the pressure for private settlement would still be great, and this does not contradict the fact that many courts are *years* behind, indicating that at least some new courts are necessary. Not until the people become more aware of this shortage will they put pressure on their legislators to create more courts and hire more judges, on both a state and national scale. The judicial branch of government has never received the kind of public financing it needs to care properly for the needs of the public.

Ignorance of the Law

A third problem is widespread ignorance of the law. Most people don't know what their rights are or when their rights are being abridged. They don't know when to go to a lawyer or how to go about getting one. Although lawyers are listed in the Yellow Pages of every telephone directory, it might be helpful if state legislatures were to establish a public information bureau to enable a person to find the right lawyer for his problem. It might also be very helpful if more schools and adult education courses were to teach at least the rudiments of the law and how the legal system works. When a person knows what is expected of him as a member of his state and nation, he will know what to do when his constitutional or legal rights have been infringed.

Disrespect for the Law

A fourth problem is disrespect for the law. The law survives only so long as people follow it. When only a few people break the law, they can be put in jail, the law is upheld and society protected. But if a great many people do not obey the law, society breaks down. A lawless society is too chaotic for decency or civilization to survive. The thought that "it's not illegal if you can get away with it" is misleading and dangerous. Whether you are caught or not, disrespect for the law is destructive of the whole fabric of our nation.

What about unjust laws? It is true that the United States itself was formed when citizens in the British colonies revolted against the unjust application of laws. Does the same philosophy apply today? If you think a law is unjust, are you free to disobey it? This question is crucial today, as thousands of people are rebelling, for the most part peacefully, against laws and conditions they consider unfair and unjust. But, if you break a law because you don't like it, you must be prepared to accept the consequences. The principle of "civil disobedience" has played a significant part in our democracy, but, generally, it has been possible to change the law by democratic means through election procedures and litigation in court. The process may be slow, but it is sure.

Perhaps the moral is clear: we can only expect the law to be observed when it first guarantees to *all* citizens equal rights and protections. And when this becomes a reality, disrespect for the law cannot be tolerated.

SOME PARTICULAR PROBLEMS OF THE CRIMINAL LAW

In recent years, hot controversy has raged over the function of criminal law and procedures. Many of the problems are interrelated: the problems of coerced confession, the right to have counsel and warning a suspect of his rights.

Is punishment, or the threat of punishment, a deterrent to crime?

Undoubtedly some people are deterred from committing crimes because they fear the consequences of being caught. Undoubtedly, too, some convicts, after serving their prison terms, do not commit further crimes because they know it isn't worth the price of going back to jail. On the other hand, a large number of crimes are committed by people who do not stop to think about the consequences. Well over half the people in prisons are "repeaters," criminals who have served time in prison prior to their present sentences. What causes crime? How can one get to the roots of crime? What else needs to be done to prevent crime?

Are our jail sentences fair?

Prior to conviction, defendants by and large (subject to some problems noted below) receive great procedural protection. The entire thrust of the constitutional law into the area of criminal procedures has been to ensure that only the really guilty are convicted. But after conviction the great safeguards seem to break down. Laws regulating the length of jail sentences vary greatly among the 50 states. In one state a convicted person may serve five years; for the same crime in another state he may be put away for 120 years. Even within the same state, the laws seem so arbitrary that they defy explanation. In one state a man who owns burglary tools can be sent to jail for 10 years; if he uses them, for only five years. In another state, a man who slips into a house through a partly opened door may get 10 years, whereas the same man, if he opens the door himself, intending to steal something once he gets inside, may be sentenced to death. Sentencing reform is urgently necessary; what kind of reform is best?

Do our prisons work?

If punishment were the sole reason for prisons, everyone might agree they work. Surely, losing your liberty is harsh punishment. But much crime is committed because the criminal is poor, has no job, and is unable to adjust to society. "Rehabilitation" (correction) of the criminal should be a very important part of the criminal law, since society is protected only so long as the prisoner is actually in jail. Unfortunately, for a long time rehabilitation was the weakest part of criminal law enforcement. Jails are crowded, uncomfortable, and dismal. Often a prisoner will learn more about crime inside a jail than he would outside. Life in jail can make a man exceedingly bitter.

A sound balance—one not yet fully realized—must be struck between jail as a correctional institution and jail as a deterrent institution. Happily, many states have realized the problem and are taking vigorous steps in the direction of providing training facilities to educate the convict for a better life once he regains his freedom.

How good is hospitalization for the insane and mentally incompetent?

Somewhat fewer than 250,000 people are serving terms in jail, but nearly 750,000 people are now confined to mental institutions. Many of them have been committed to the institution for a crime. In many states, a defendant can avoid a jail sentence if he can establish that he is "mentally incompetent" to stand trial, to serve his sentence, or because he suffered from some mental defect at the time he committed the offense with which he is charged. But many mental hospitals are very much like prisons. Because of a lack of funds and skilled and dedicated people (in large part due to public ignorance of the problem and inadequate salaries), many mental patients languish their lives away in crowded, uncomfortable buildings lacking in privacy. These institutions do not deserve to be called hospitals. This is not true everywhere; there *are* good mental hospitals, but unfortunately far too few.

The problems concerning "hospital vs. jail" are numerous: should a commission composed of expert psychiatrists decide on when to send a defendant to a hospital rather than have a judge preside over a jury trial with all the protections of the constitutional law? Can mentally incompetent persons be sent away before they have done anything wrong? Many are. (Compare your answer to that question with your answer to this one: can a man be put in jail before he has committed a crime?)

Is it fair to deny mental patients the rights to use the telephone or to write or receive letters? Sometimes patients are denied these rights. How long a time should a patient be made to spend in a hospital, especially one where he is receiving little treatment? What methods can be devised for ensuring that his case is reviewed by courts every so often to determine whether he should be released? How can a mentally incompetent person defend himself? Who will speak out for such a person? And what do we mean when we speak of mentally incompetent: mentally incompetent for what? Only recently has the whole problem of mental institutions and the criminal law begun to be explored.

How fair is our bail system?

Bail is supposed to ensure that the defendant who is allowed to wait for his trial outside jail will actually come to trial. It also is supposed to protect society from the danger that the defendant will commit another crime before the trial. The theory is that the defendant will not want to forfeit a large sum of money. But in practice, many defendants raise bail by advancing a relatively small sum of money to the professional bail bondsmen (who themselves sometimes make exorbitant profits). A defendant might be willing to forfeit this smaller sum. A more aggravated problem occurs with indigent defendants: many courts say that if a man has just enough money to pay bail *or* to hire a lawyer, he must choose between his freedom or his "right" to counsel; he cannot have both. Is this fair? Is it constitutional?

How can we stop the police from coercing confessions?

For the most part, confession by torture does not happen any more (though the danger must ever be guarded against). More subtle means of coercion are used all the time, however. Prolonged questioning periods, frightening a suspect, not advising him of his rights—all contribute to the coercion. Coercion can be eliminated by effectively warning the suspect of his rights, by providing counsel, and by refusing to admit the confession into evidence if it is found to be coerced. But how can coercion be proved? Moreover, suppose the confession is true. Should its use be disallowed because the police acted unconstitutionally, even though it proved the suspect guilty?

What is more important: putting a guilty man behind bars or making sure the police obey the laws too? The Supreme Court has answered in recent years that both are of equal importance and that the police will have to find ways other than coercion to gather evidence to convict. The police argue that they will be severely hampered in their law-enforcement activities. Others (and some police included) argue that protection of constitutional rights is of paramount importance, and legal methods can and will be found.

How should a suspect be effectively advised of which rights?

In many communities, perhaps in most, arrested persons are *not* warned of all their constitutional rights—of their right to remain silent, of their right to counsel, or of the fact that anything they say can be used against them in evidence at trial. In June, 1966, the Supreme Court said it would be *unconstitutional* for the police not to inform a suspect of all these rights *before* questioning him. How can we insure that the suspect be *effectively* informed of these rights?

At what point and for what crimes does a defendant deserve a lawyer?

The Supreme Court also ruled in 1966 that the right to counsel begins as soon as the suspect is arrested. If he cannot afford a lawyer, the state must hire one for him. Where will all the lawyers come from? Suppose the arrest occurs at night time, when no lawyers are immediately available, and the police have to question the suspect to prevent possible further crime from occurring right then. Must they refrain from questioning the suspect until he consults his lawyer? How can lawyers be made immediately available? For what crimes are lawyers necessary? All crimes? Only felonies?

Should a judge exclude evidence illegally seized?

Suppose the police, without probable cause, break into a house to see what they can find, and discover narcotics. Can the narcotics be used at the trial? (Unauthorized possession of narcotics is a crime.) Can the policy testify as to what they found, when what they did was clearly unconstitutional? The Supreme Court a few years ago said such evidence could not be used, nor, if the police are led to further evidence because of the illegally seized evidence, can they use the further evidence. They are said not to be allowed to use the "fruit of the poisonous tree." But how far should this doctrine go? Suppose the police illegally stumble on a gang's preparation for a major crime? Is there no way by which they can prevent that crime or bring the criminals to trial?

Should newspapers be allowed to report and discuss indictments and unproved accusations?

When a man is indicted by a grand jury, he is not necessarily guilty. Yet, there is a tendency on the part of the newspapers and the public to act as though indictment is proof of guilt. Sometimes juries have been known to convict an innocent person because of what they have read in the newspapers. Moreover, the publicity given many criminal trials in which the accused is found innocent can seriously injure a person's later life.

How can a fair trial be guaranteed? The newspaper's right to publish is itself guaranteed by the First Amendment to the Constitution. Any law which tried to prevent a newspaper from printing an article about a trial would be unconstitutional. Some judges, lawyers, and law-enforcement officers have suggested that one way to solve the "fair trial—free comment" problem is to put sanctions (see page 51) on lawyers and officials who make comments to newspapers about a pending case. In other words, freedom of press will not be curbed; only the non-constitutionally protected "right" to talk about the trial will be muffled.

But don't the newspapers have a point when they say that it will then be difficult for them to carry out the important public task of inquiring into how fairly the trial is being carried out by the police, judge, and lawyers when they can't get the information they need?

A PERSONAL PROBLEM FOR THE LAWYER

Although usually the legal profession is highly esteemed, it is unfortunately true that some unscrupulous lawyers give a bad name to their fellows. The problem is an old one. Shakespeare recognized it when he had Dick the Butcher say in a line from *Henry VI* (Part 2, Act 4, Scene 2): "The first thing we do, let's kill all the lawyers." Because lawyers are specialists who know the law and are often at the center of power, they are sometimes feared. Their decisions and recommendations can have tremendous influence in shaping the institutions of our society.

As with any profession, some decisions pose ethical problems for judges and lawyers. These problems are sometimes acute. For instance, when a lawyer is conducting his client's case at trial, how can he be (and should he be) stopped from asking questions in order to suggest conclusions to the jury? Since the law is an adversary system, we may conclude that his job is only to fight for his client; protecting the other party is, after all, what the judge and opposing counsel are there for. On the other hand, if a lawyer goes too far and asks "improper" questions, he may lose on appeal, or a mistrial may be declared and he will have to start all over, or his client may lose altogether. More drastic yet, his license to practice law may be suspended or revoked. But far more serious is the effect which improper practices may have on the legal system. Can the average person hope to find justice in a system in which lawyers are themselves not living up to the law?

Possible ethical conflicts which may confront the lawyer range from the trivial to the enormous. Deliberately asking one improper question at a trial may be trivial. What does the lawyer do, on the other hand, when a person comes to him for advice on what is the best way to commit a crime? The lawyer is under a moral duty to keep the confidence of his clients. Suppose the lawyer strongly advises the person not to commit the crime, and the person says he'll think it over? Can the lawyer alert the police—legally? ethically?

Some of these questions are answered by the "legal canons of ethics," a body of moral rules which lawyers by and large are obliged to follow. But many of the rules are vague and some are not obeyed by anyone because the profession as a whole disagrees with the committee of the bar which wrote them.

None of these problems—general problems in the judicial system, problems in the administration of criminal law, ethical problems confronting lawyers—can be quickly solved, because new twists and new problems always crop up. Although our political, judicial, educational, and religious leaders are grappling with these issues it is not at all unsafe to suggest that it is the coming generation of lawyers and other leaders who will ultimately have the responsibility of solving them. Certainly the problems will be with us when those now in school come to face them. They call for the highest use of creative energy, skill, patience, and diligence.

A Harvard Law School professor illustrates his point on a warm spring day.

Part VIII: Careers in the Law

It is often said that a legal education is a good background for doing anything. Although this statement should not be taken literally, it is, nevertheless, true that training in law is often a springboard for both men and women to opportunities in many different careers. (Today there are 7,000 women lawyers.) Let us find out how you can become a lawyer and see what a lawyer's job is like.

THE LAW SCHOOL

Requirements

In every state, some kind of legal education is necessary before you can become a lawyer. Except in rare cases, if you want to be a lawyer, you must go to law school. American law schools almost universally require three years for the bachelor of laws degree (the L.L.B.). Law schools range in size from a few dozen people per class in the smaller ones, to more than 520 students per class at the Harvard Law School.

Among the entrance requirements at most law schools is a college of diploma. In addition, you will probably have to take the "law boards," a private exam designed to test your reasoning ability, administered by Educational Testing Service, the same organization which gives the College Board exams. Your relative score on the law boards (determined by comparing your score with that of everyone else taking the test at the same time) is often considered an important factor by law school admission committees. The cost of a legal education varies, depending on the school. Increasingly, scholarships and loans are being made available to deserving students who cannot afford the whole cost themselves.

Courses

The largest part of your work throughout the three years in law school will be reading and discussing actual cases already decided by the courts. Law textbooks are called "casebooks" because they consist of 1,000 pages of the most important cases in the field. In the criminal law course, for instance, you will actually read Mr. Justice Black's opinion in *Gideon v. Wainwright* (holding that the state must provide you with defense counsel if you request one and are too poor to afford your own). In your constitutional law course, you will read, among hundreds of others, Chief Justice Warren's opinion in *Brown v. Board of Education* (the school desegregation case) and *Reynolds v. Sims* (the legislative reapportionment case). By the time you finish law school, you will have read thousands of cases.

Perhaps only 15 pages per night will be assigned per course, but it is more difficult than it sounds. Legal opinions are often dense, and you must become well acquainted with the facts and holdings of each case because the professor might call on you the next day in class to "state the case" (briefly tell the class who is suing whom, why, what the facts are, what the legal arguments are, the holding, and the judge's reasons for so holding). The professor will then ask

UNITED STATES *v.* BROWN.

CERTIORARI TO THE UNITED STATES COURT OF APPEALS FOR
THE NINTH CIRCUIT.

No. 399. Argued March 29, 1965.—Decided June 7, 1965.

Respondent was convicted under § 504 of the Labor-Management
Reporting and Disclosure Act of 1959, which makes it a crime for
one who belongs to the Communist Party or who has been a member thereof during the preceding five years wilfully to serve as a
member of the executive board of a labor organization. The Court
of Appeals reversed, holding § 504 violative of the First and Fifth
Amendments. *Held:* Section 504 constitutes a bill of attainder
and is therefore unconstitutional. Pp. 441–462.

(a) The Bill of Attainder Clause, Art. I, § 9, cl. 3, was intended
to implement the separation of powers among the three branches
of the Government by guarding against the legislative exercise of
judicial power. Pp. 441–446.

(b) The Bill of Attainder Clause is to be liberally construed in
the light of its purpose to prevent legislative punishment of designated persons or groups. *Cummings* v. *Missouri,* 4 Wall. 277;
Ex parte Garland, 4 Wall. 333; *United States* v. *Lovett,* 328 U. S.
303. Pp. 447–449.

(c) In designating Communist Party members as those persons
who cannot hold union office, Congress has exceeded its Commerce
Clause power to enact generally applicable legislation disqualifying from positions affecting interstate commerce persons who may
use such positions to cause political strikes. Pp. 449–452.

(d) Section 504 is distinguishable from such conflict-of-interest
statutes as § 32 of the Banking Act, where Congress was legislating
with respect to general characteristics rather than with respect to
the members of a specific group. Pp. 453–455.

(e) The designation of Communist Party membership cannot
be justified as an alternative, "shorthand" expression for the characteristics which render men likely to incite political strikes. Pp.
455–456.

(f) A statute which inflicts its deprivation upon named or
described persons or groups constitutes a bill of attainder whether
its aim is retributive, punishing past acts, or preventive, discouraging future conduct. In *American Communications Assn.* v. *Douds,*
339 U. S. 382, where the Court upheld § 9 (h) of the National

The first page of the official Supreme Court reports contains the head notes.

Labor Relations Act, the predecessor of § 504, the Court erroneously assumed that only a law visiting retribution for past acts could constitute a bill of attainder, and misread the statute involved in *United States* v. *Lovett.* 328 U. S. 303, which it sought to distinguish from § 9 (h), as being in that category. Pp. 456–460.

(g) The legislative specification of those to whom the enacted sanction is to apply invalidates a provision as a bill of attainder whether the individuals are designated by name as in *Lovett* or by description as here. Pp. 461–462.

334 F. 2d 488, affirmed.

Solicitor General Cox argued the cause for the United States. With him on the brief were *Assistant Attorney General Yeagley, Nathan Lewin, Kevin T. Maroney* and *George B. Searls.*

Richard Gladstein argued the cause for respondent. With him on the brief was *Norman Leonard.*

Briefs of *amici curiae,* urging affirmance, were filed by *Melvin L. Wulf* for the American Civil Liberties Union of Northern California et al., and by *Victor Rabinowitz* and *Leonard B. Boudin* for the Emergency Civil Liberties Committee.

MR. CHIEF JUSTICE WARREN delivered the opinion of the Court.

In this case we review for the first time a conviction under § 504 of the Labor-Management Reporting and Disclosure Act of 1959, which makes it a crime for a member of the Communist Party to serve as an officer or (except in clerical or custodial positions) as an employee of a labor union.[1] Section 504, the purpose of which is to protect

---

[1] 73 Stat. 519, 536, 29 U. S. C. § 504 (1958 ed., Supp. IV). The section, which took effect on September 14, 1959, provides, in pertinent part:

"(a) No person who is or has been a member of the Communist Party . . . shall serve—

"(1) as an officer, director, trustee, member of any executive board or similar governing body, business agent, manager, organizer, or other

---

The opinion itself begins on the next.

questions about the case, not only to test your knowledge but also to learn whether you thought the judge was right or wrong. It is essential to be prepared each day or you will not benefit from the class discussion. And discussion is perhaps more important than reading, for through talk and debate you can test your ideas against those of your professor and fellow students. Remember, after all, that this is precisely what goes on when a lawyer argues a case on appeal before appellate judges.

There are many treatises and reference books, in addition to casebooks, which will aid you in understanding the law. Perhaps the most famous of these is a set of one-volume books known as the "Hornbook" series, issued by a commercial publisher. The Hornbooks are valuable reference tools and are written by some of the most eminent lawyers and teachers in the field.

You will be required to take courses in torts, contracts, criminal law, civil procedure, property, and constitutional law. You will probably take courses in evidence, taxation, corporations, commercial transactions, and administrative law. You may find a whole range of courses to suit your interests: labor law, antitrust law, international law, jurisprudence, copyright law, and many others. In most schools you will be tested in your courses only at the final examination. Usually no papers are required, although some schools require an essay in the third year, and some assign a research topic in the first year in order to teach the student the techniques of legal research.

Moot Court

A required activity, however, is the "moot court" competition. A moot court is one in which courtroom procedures are duplicated in order to give practice in arguing cases. You will be given a set of facts (which might be fictitious or based on an actual case), and you will have to research the law and write a brief. Your opposing counsel will prepare his case in the same manner, and on a certain day you will appear before judges (usually advanced students and professors) and argue the case just as though it were real.

In many schools, the moot court competition extends for three years. The winners (those who receive the highest scores for their briefs and arguments) of each round of cases argue more difficult cases in succeeding rounds, until finally only four are left. The two teams then argue before a panel of distinguished judges, sometimes, at some law schools, even a United States Supreme Court Justice. Winning the final argument, or even achieving the final stage of a moot court competition is one of the highest honors at law school.

The "Law Review"

Another high honor is being elected an editor of the "law review" or "law journal." A law review is a professional journal devoted to discussion of the latest developments in all fields of the law. Usually only a small number of students, chosen solely on the basis of grades, can work on the journal. In every other profession, the professional journals are edited by professionals already working in the field. Law is the only profession in which the major publications are edited by students. Most articles are written by law professors, lawyers, or judges, although the students often write "notes" or "comments" on recent cases or particular aspects of the law.

THE BAR

You do not automatically become a lawyer fit to practice before "the bar" after you graduate from law school. (The "bar" in English courtrooms—in many American courtrooms, too—is a long metal railing separating the general public from the area where the lawyers argue.) In order to practice law in your state you must first pass the "bar examination." This is an exam given by the state "board of bar examiners" to test your knowledge of the state's laws and legal procedures, for obviously it is essential that a lawyer know the law of his state well.

Surprisingly enough, many law school graduates do not feel equipped to take the bar examination right away. At many law schools, more attention is paid to general principles of law than to the actual tort or contract or property doctrines of any one state, so graduates take a "bar review" or "bar refresher" course, to learn the specific rules of law and procedure of their state, sometimes in as short a period as 6 weeks or less.

Once you pass the bar examination you must appear before the board of bar examiners, who will question you concerning your moral fitness to be a lawyer. If you have been in legal trouble earlier in your life you may not satisfy the requirement of fitness. But almost all who pass the written exam are "admitted to the bar."

A member of the bar in one state usually cannot practice law in another state unless he has been admitted to that state's bar. In order to practice in the federal courts, you must be admitted to a separate federal bar. In order to argue before the United States Supreme Court, you must have been admitted to practice before your state supreme court first.

The Bar Association

The bar and the state bar association are not always the same thing. The bar association is composed only of lawyers and judges within the state, but anyone who has been admitted to the bar may become a member. Sometimes a social group, a bar association also has committees which explore problems of the law within their state. They adopt "canons of ethics," sets of ethical rules which a lawyer is obliged to follow. If he breaches a canon of ethics, a committee of the bar association may recommend he be disbarred; an attorney may only be disbarred by a court after an official hearing. "Disbarring" means an attorney loses his license to practice law, and can be fined or jailed if he continues to practice.

Any person who practices law (gives legal advice) but who is not a member of the bar is liable to fine or imprisonment. In about half the states, a lawyer *must* (according to law) be a member of the bar association.

There is also the national association, the American Bar Association. Membership in the A.B.A. is not necessary to practice law, but about one-half of all lawyers in the country belong. The A.B.A. has many important committees which report on various topics of the law and recommend changes.

A related group, the American Law Institute, is responsible for drafting many model laws, such as the Model Penal Code. This is a code which the lawyers and judges of the American Law Institute believe would be better than the existing set of criminal statutes in the states and which would, if adopted by the state legislatures, make for uniformity in criminal law throughout the country. The A.L.I. also publishes many-volumed works summarizing the laws of contracts, torts, property, and other fields. These are called "Restatements" (e.g., The Restatement of the Law of Torts). Although these are not binding on courts, judges sometimes give weight to the black-letter statements of the law and the explanations and examples given in the Restatements.

Still other private lawyers' groups draft other kinds of codes. One is the Uniform Commercial Code, which has now been adopted by more than 40 states.

LAW PRACTICE

Having been admitted to the bar, you might go into private practice for yourself. More than 200,000 lawyers of the total 300,000 licensed attorneys in the U.S. today are in private practice. You could open up an office, put your

name on the door, and wait for clients to come to you. The canons of legal ethics forbid you to advertise, so you would have to wait for the word to spread that you were open for business.

The Law Firm

Usually, however, you would go to work for an already existing law firm, at least for a few years, to gain experience. (After that you might go into practice for yourself. Most lawyers still work singly, with neither partners nor lawyer employees.) Law firms are associations of lawyers. A few of the lawyers are the "partners" of the firm. They control and direct the firm and its policies. Other lawyers are paid a yearly salary to work for the firm and they are usually called "associates." Law firms come in all sizes, from very small, two-man firms to huge metropolitan firms with more than 100 lawyers.

Some firms carry on a "general practice," that is, they take almost any kind of client and case which comes to them. They handle automobile accidents, write construction contracts, draft wills, take divorce cases, form corporations, and argue tax cases. Other firms specialize in certain fields. One firm may carry on an extensive trial practice. It will take mostly the kinds of cases which eventually will go to trial. Often these firms are exclusively tort firms or general business law firms.

Some of the large city firms may deal exclusively with corporation and tax laws. Lawyers in this kind of firm will spend most of their time advising their clients about corporation law, or about ways in which to earn and spend money so as legally to pay less income tax. Or they may spend the bulk of their time drafting contracts and helping to negotiate with other companies.

Some firms specialize entirely in "estate planning." The way an estate— whether personal or real property—is disposed of in a will can often be very important for tax and other purposes. Inheritance and tax laws are extremely tricky, and if an estate is to be disposed of properly, it is necessary to have a lawyer draft the will. Similarly, mortgaging and transactions concerning property in general (such as the sale of land), necessitate legal advice. There are firms which specialize in giving that advice.

There are also firms which specialize in labor law, some working closely with management, others with unions. A specialized knowledge of labor law and the workings of the National Labor Relations Board is crucial. Law firms deal with "securities" (stocks and bonds), with radio and television communication laws, with copyrights and patents, with theater and the arts, with transportation problems, and with criminal law. Some firms deal only with cases coming up in their state courts; some firms exclusively handle cases in the federal courts.

There are many other kinds of specialties. In fact, wherever there is a special court, industry or business, there will probably be a specialized law firm to help.

OTHER AREAS OF PRACTICE

A lawyer need not work for a law firm or maintain a private practice. He may join the staff of a corporation. Many business companies and corporations have their own legal departments to handle their special problems of contracts, etc. These lawyers are known as "house counsel"; some 20,000 lawyers are so employed.

A lawyer will also find thousands of job opportunities in government service.

From the local municipal agencies to the state government agencies, to the Congress and federal executive departments, lawyers are in demand. Since government—any government in the United States—derives its authority solely from the law, lawyers are needed to guide its many actions. More than 40,000 lawyers are employed by government agencies, and the number of positions is sure to grow.

Legal Fees

Most lawyers in private practice do not receive a fixed salary. They are paid fees by their clients. The size of the fee depends on the kind of case, the amount of time it took, how difficult it was, what the chances of winning were originally thought to be, and how much the client can afford to pay. Some lawyers, on the other hand, are paid a fixed yearly salary; for instance, those who work for law firms but who are not partners. The partners divide among themselves the profits earned by the firm, after deducting as costs such items as the salaries of non-partners. The law can be a lucrative business, and for very prominent lawyers incomes in excess of $100,000 yearly are not unknown.

Public Defenders

Since the holding in the *Gideon* case that the state must provide each indigent defendant in a criminal case with defense counsel and pay for his fees, some states and local communities have established an office of "public defender." The public defender, like the prosecutor, is an official of the state or local government but he is paid to fight on behalf of defendants. His job is to search for evidence supporting the clients who have been assigned to his office by the court, and to argue against the prosecutor during the trial. Only a minority of communities have public defenders today, but it is thought that their adoption will grow.

THE JUDGE

For many lawyers, the highest achievement of the legal profession is to become a judge. But there is no sure route to attaining this goal. In proportion to the number of lawyers, the number of judges is small. All federal judges are appointed by the President; one way to become a judge, therefore, is to know or be known to the President. More often, a lawyer will be recommended by the United States Senator from his state. Sometimes, the quality of lawyer's work and his writing attract the attention of the President and his advisors, among them the Attorney General. Usually, the higher court judges and Supreme Court justices have been political leaders, outstanding lower federal court or state court judges, and have otherwise been distinguished in public life.

Federal judges are appointed for life terms and their salaries cannot constitutionally be diminished while they are in office. They can be removed from office only by "impeachment" (formal accusation) and conviction by the United States Congress. A federal judge cannot be removed by being impeached unless he deviates from the standard of "good behavior," and this generally means committing a crime or a grossly immoral act.

State judges are often elected, but usually they must be approved (by custom but not by law) by the state bar association. Federal judges, too, are usually nominated by the President only if approved by the American Bar Association, which maintains a committee for that purpose. Although the terms of state judges are often less than life, they are usually eligible for re-election. To have the public elect judges has been criticized on the grounds that the qualifications of a good judge cannot be determined and analyzed by the electorate and that a judge should not have to make his decisions on the meaning of the law conform to popular likes and tastes. State impeachment procedures sometimes differ from those in the federal system, but by and large, in the state as well as in the federal judiciaries, a judgeship is a secure job.

OFFICERS OF THE COURT

Although judges are primarily recognized as carrying the burden of ensuring that justice is done, within the judiciary the work of the court cannot be done by them alone. Those who are also responsible for the administration of justice within the judicial system are sometimes referred to as "officers of the court." These include lawyers and police officers, as well as those who are paid to work for the court. Lawyers and police are said to owe a duty not only to their clients or their city or political leaders, but also to the cause of justice. There are some things they are not supposed to do while representing their side in court, such as tampering with the evidence, for instance. Their cause should be the truth, even more than winning the case for their clients. This dual role often leads to conflict when, for instance, a lawyer is defending a man he thinks is guilty. The dual role makes the job interesting but difficult.

Here, however, we will consider briefly the jobs of those whose work is done directly for the court.

Clerk of the Court

Much of the administrative paper work is handled by the clerk of the court. The keeping of the judicial calendars, the recording of the judgments, the actual notifications of one sort or another sent out by the court, are the work of the clerk. He does not, however, make decisions affecting the parties. He carries out the orders of the judges.

Sometimes his task is simple. For instance, when the court decides a case, the judges do not usually write the actual judgment. The winning lawyer drafts the wording of the judgment. If it is in accordance with the holding of the court, the losing party will agree to it, and the clerk will merely add the official seal of the court and enter it in the official books. If the parties do not agree on the form of the judgment, the clerk will report this to the judges and the court will prepare the document.

Sometimes the work of the clerk is more complex. When motions for appeal come to the court, the clerk must keep track of them, schedule the hearings should the judges order them, and send for the transcripts and other records of the trials. If it is a trial court, the clerk must keep a record of the evidence. He must deal with the opposing attorneys and schedule all hearings before the judges and trials before juries.

In short, the clerk must keep under control all the day-to-day activities of the court.

The Reporter

The court reporter is responsible for the publication of all the opinions and decisions of the court. In his hands lies the accuracy of the citations and each page of the reports. The reporter also writes the "head notes." These are the notes that appear at the beginning of each case summarizing briefly the holdings in the case. The reporter must be a trained and skilled lawyer who can devote considerable attention to the detail of each case. In many courts assistant reporters aid the reporter in his work.

The Law Clerk

The law clerk is, perhaps, not technically an officer of the court. He works not for the court as a whole, but as a judge's only personal assistant. The job is not usually a career one. It is often held by recent honor graduates of law schools, who come to learn much about the inner workings of a court, about legal research, and about the ways in which judges make legal decisions. Most judges have one law clerk; some choose more. The law clerk has a great deal of work to do—mostly researching the law of the cases which the judge must decide, and discussing legal points with the judge. Occasionally law clerks write the basic draft of an opinion. Although sometimes a lawyer will "clerk" no more than two years (and will often stay for only one year), the job of judge's law clerk is a vitally important one to both the state and federal judiciary.

The Receiver

To secure complete justice for both parties, it is often necessary to have a neutral party direct the affairs of a company or estate in litigation. The person who does this (the "receiver," so called because he receives the property from the court) is responsible for carrying out the directions of the court. He may have to pay off a company's debts. He may have to keep a company in operation. Some major railroads, for instance, for a number of years have been in the hands of receivers. Receivers deal with many different kinds of property; for example, jewelry, hotels, steamboats, grain in warehouses, wild animals, a secret information code, theaters, and patents have all been entrusted to receivers by courts.

Special Guardians

Sometimes children have interests which have to be protected by courts. For instance, a child may have inherited money from relatives, which his parents are spending. Or a child, after being in an accident, may have desperate need of a blood transfusion, but his parents refuse to allow it for religious reasons. Since the child is powerless to help himself, a court will appoint someone—often a lawyer—to be his "special guardian" to ensure that the child keeps his money, or his life.

Referees and Masters

Sometimes in complex cases, a court needs specific information and does not have the time to obtain it. It may need to know the financial condition of a company, or what happened at the scene of an accident. To get the needed information, the court will appoint a disinterested person to act as "referee" or "master" (sometimes, "master in equity"). This person will gather the evidence, or track down the persons, ask the questions and write up the answers, often giving his opinion as to whether the answers can be believed. Many administrative boards have an Examiner or Trial Examiner, whose job is to uncover the facts of the case pending before the Board; most commonly he obtains the facts by holding hearings, and makes a report of his findings and recommendations to the judge.

Committees for Incompetents

There are some unfortunate people who are not competent to care for themselves: they may be physically ill for a long period of time, feeble-minded, or mentally ill. A court will appoint a guardian or a committee of guardians to care for such incompetent persons. Because lawyers can deal best with legal problems and are known to the judges, they are often appointed to these responsible positions. (Unlike other officers of the court, receivers, referees, guardians, and committees for incompetents are not *permanent* officers; different individuals are appointed on a temporary basis whenever the need arises.)

Other Officers

There are many other officers of the court.

The STENOGRAPHER takes down with a special shorthand machine (a "steno-type") everything which is said during the trial. These notes are then typed and become the permanent court record, to be used by the lawyers, the judge, and the appellate courts.

The BAILIFF is in charge of the jury. It is his duty to ensure that the jury can deliberate in private. He may also perform duties which in many states the SHERIFF performs: the attachment of property for sale at judicial auctions, and the disposition of private property which comes into the hands of the court because of a lawsuit.

Among his other duties, the MARSHAL is responsible for keeping order in the courtroom and attending to the personnel of the court.

LEGAL SECRETARY

The secretary in a law office must be more than an ordinary executive secretary. Shorthand and typing skills are of course necessary, but in addition she should have some legal knowledge and familiarity with legal terms. The legal secretary does more than simply answer correspondence; she types long legal forms and documents with great accuracy. Because she is skilled, a good legal secretary is always in demand and commands a relatively high salary.

LEGAL PUBLISHERS

A number of publishing houses devote a large part of their time to the publication of legal books. They publish reports of most state and federal cases, and may even publish the complete laws of every state and the United States, including "annotated statutes." A set of annotated statutes contains court interpretations of the meaning of the various clauses. Since these interpretations are as much a part of the law as the statutes themselves, it is essential to use them when "looking up the law." These companies also publish hundreds of legal treatises, encyclopedias, and other vital reference materials. One publication is a more-than-100-volume set of books containing thousands of pages of nothing but numbers! It is called *Shepard's Citations*, and is invaluable in that it enables the lawyer and judge to see what cases have been referred to by courts in other cases. The publication of all these books is a vast enterprise and the publishers need law-trained editors and others for a number of different kinds of jobs.

LAW PROFESSORS

The teaching of law can be a hectic but rewarding profession. Because he has specialized training, the law professor draws a salary higher than teachers in many other fields. By being at a university, he can profit from discussions with fellow professors and pursue whatever research he is interested in. In addition, many law professors profit monetarily by carrying on a law consultation practice, too.

A law degree is necessary in order to teach law, although an advanced legal degree is usually not (in contrast to many academic fields in which the Ph.D. degree is often necessary). Most teachers are required to have a few years of experience as a working lawyer before becoming a professor.

LEGAL JOURNALISTS

The profession of "legal journalist" (one who specializes in reporting the law for newspapers, magazines, radio, or TV) is a new one. There are only a few newspapers which hire a full-time legal specialist for their reporting staff. But because the law can be very complicated at times, more and more newspapers and other news media have realized that a legally-trained reporter can be a valuable staff man.

LAW-ENFORCEMENT OFFICERS

There are a number of jobs concerned with the enforcement of the law. Such jobs include the police, district attorneys, and investigators for the Federal Bureau of Investigation (F.B.I.). A large part of their work consists of detecting violations of the criminal law, whether federal or state, and prosecuting offenders.

The F.B.I. is under the jurisdiction of the United States Department of Justice. The Attorney General of the United States, who heads the department, is a cabinet officer and the chief law-enforcement agent of the nation. His department is in charge, among other things, of prosecuting all violations of federal criminal laws and prosecuting civil antitrust suits. For instance, when a company acts in possible restraint of trade laws the Attorney General will ask the court for an injunction against the company. The U.S. Attorney and his staff serve as the agents of the Attorney General in each judicial district of the United States.

In addition to directing all the divisions of the Justice Department, the Attorney General acts as chief legal adviser to the President. Whenever the President needs a legal opinion on action he wants to take, or on bills he wants to submit to Congress or signs, it is the Attorney General's responsibility to make sure that they are drafted carefully and constitutionally. The Attorney General is also largely responsible for selecting candidates for nomination to judicial office.

Directly under the United States Attorney General is the Solicitor General of the United States. Whenever the United States is a plaintiff or defendant to a suit before the Supreme Court the Solicitor General or one of his staff will argue the case (unless the Attorney General himself appears). Often the Solicitor General will appear even though the United States is not a party to the suit. Any federal court may ask the Solicitor General to submit a brief or appear in person in order to advise the court of the legal opinion of the United

States Government in the matter at hand. When the Solicitor General does so, he is said to appear as an "amicus curiae," or friend of the court.

The United States Department of Justice has other divisions, aside from the criminal division which contains the F.B.I. and the office of the Solicitor General. These other offices include the civil rights division, the antitrust division, and the internal security division (dealing with subversion within the country).

Each state has an executive department headed by an attorney general. The state attorney general's function is quite similar to the job of the U.S. Attorney General: the executive watchdog over the law enforcement process.

PUBLIC OFFICE

The profession most significantly represented in elected public office is the law. In 1965, five members of the President's Cabinet, 67 United States Senators, and a majority of the House of Representatives were lawyers. The proportion of lawyers who are governors and who are members of state houses is often as high. Because the elected official deals directly with law—either making it or enforcing it—and because if he loses the next election he can always go back to practicing law, the lawyer is often attracted to public service.

INDEX

111

resting case, 34
restitution, 50
restraints on Supreme Court, 76
retroactive law, 47
reversing jury, 55
reviewing case, 14
revocation, 45
Reynolds v. Sims, 75
right to counsel, 26, 87
robbery, 36
rule, 15
rules of decision, Supreme Court, 76

sanctions, 51–53
sentence, 46
, suspended, 52
service of summons, 11
settlement of dispute, 10
Shepard's Citations, 104
sheriff, 103
Sixteenth Amendment, 76
Sixth Amendment, 26, 29
small claims court, 63
Solicitor General of United States, 93, 105
special guardians, 102
verdict, 56
specific performance, 43, 49
stare decisis, 16
state courts, 63–66
jurisdiction, 68
supreme, 65
Statute of Frauds, 43
statute, 14
of limitations, 53
statutory suit, 48
strict liability, 41
substantial performance, 45
suit, on judgment, 71
, prohibitions against, 53
, statutory, 48

summary judgment, 12, 13–14
summing up, 35
summons, 11
superior court, 65
Supreme Court of the United States, 72–81
supreme court of states, 65
suspect, 23
suspended sentence, 52

tax court, 62
temporary restraining order, 49
third degree, 25
torts, 40–42
, revolution in law of, 47
trespass, 41
trial, 31–39
, new, 55
, speedy and public, 29

unconstitutional laws, number of, 74
Uniform Commercial Code, 96
unilateral contract, 45
unjust laws, 84
unwritten law, 15
United States Supreme Court, 72–81
United States v. Brown, 92–93

venue, change of, 38
verdict, 37
, directed, 55
, special, 56
voir dire, 30

warrant, 24
weight of evidence, 55
Williston's *Contracts*, 17
witness, conclusion of, 31
, examination of, 31
, hostile, 34
, leading the, 32
writ of mandamus, 72
written contract, 43